Penguin Handbooks

The Ridgeway Path

Hugh Westacott was born in Londo[...]
Surrey, on the outbreak of the war. [...]
School, Kingston-upon-Thames, a[...]
Polytechnic. He was for ten years th[...]
Buckinghamshire and has also worked as a librarian in Sutton,
Croydon, Sheffield, Bradford and Brookline, Massachusetts.
During the war he spent his holidays with his family in Colyton,
east Devon, walking five miles to the sea and back again each day,
and his love of walking stems from these experiences. He is now a
freelance writer and lecturer and in 1979 he was commissioned by
Penguin to write this series of footpath guides to every national
park and official long-distance path. He has also written *The
Walker's Handbook* (Penguin, second edition 1980) and two
forthcoming books, *Long Distance Paths: An International
Directory* and *The Backpacker's Bible*. His other interests include
the history of the Royal Navy in the eighteenth century and the
writings of Evelyn Waugh. Hugh Westacott is married and has two
daughters.

Mark Richards was born in 1949 in Chipping Norton, Oxfordshire.
He was educated at Burford Grammar School before training for a
farming career. He discovered the pleasures of hill walking through
a local mountaineering club. He became friends with Alfred
Wainwright, the creator of a unique series of pictorial guides to the
fells of northern England, who encouraged him to produce a guide
to the Cotswold Way, which was followed by guides to the North
Cornish Coast Path and Offa's Dyke Path. For two years he
produced a selection of hill walks for the *Climber and Rambler*
magazine, and more recently he has contributed articles and
illustrations to the *Great Outdoors* magazine and numerous walking
books, culminating in the present series of Penguin footpath
guides. As a member of various conservation organizations and a
voluntary warden of the Cotswolds Area of Outstanding Natural
Beauty, he is interested in communicating the need for the
protection of environmental and community characteristics,
particularly in rural areas. Mark Richards is happily married with
two lively children, Alison and Daniel.

The Ridgeway Path

H. D. Westacott

With maps by Mark Richards

Penguin Books

For Mark Richards,
in appreciation

Penguin Books Ltd, Harmondsworth, Middlesex, England
Penguin Books, 625 Madison Avenue, New York, New York 10022, U.S.A.
Penguin Books Australia Ltd, Ringwood, Victoria, Australia
Penguin Books Canada Ltd, 2801 John Street, Markham, Ontario, Canada L3R 1B4
Penguin Books (N.Z.) Ltd, 182–190 Wairau Road, Auckland 10, New Zealand

First published 1982

Text copyright © H. D. Westacott, 1982
Maps copyright © Mark Richards, 1982
All rights reserved

Made and printed in Great Britain by
Richard Clay (The Chaucer Press) Ltd, Bungay, Suffolk
Set in Monophoto Univers

Contents

Acknowledgements

My thanks are due to the helpful staff of the Countryside Commission, who always give unstintingly of their time; the staff of the county libraries of Buckinghamshire, Hertfordshire, Oxfordshire and Wiltshire, for providing much helpful information; and the staff of the County Engineer's Department, Buckinghamshire, for allowing me to use their definitive maps and providing information about diversions. I am grateful, too, for all those who have written to make corrections and suggestions to the original survey published under the imprint Footpath Publications. Clare and John Mortin very kindly walked the whole route and checked the location of waymarks and signposts. The faults are mine alone.

As usual, I am particularly indebted to the skill and artistry of Mark Richards, who has drawn the superb maps. He has an instinctive eye for the essential features which will help the walker to find the route and I am extremely grateful for the many valuable suggestions that he has made. The maps are based on the 1:25000 Ordnance Survey maps, with the sanction of the Controller of Her Majesty's Stationery Office (Crown copyright reserved).

Sue Baylis has typed the manuscript with her customary accuracy and efficiency.

Introduction

The Ridgeway Path (long-distance path A2) runs for 89 miles from Overton Hill near Avebury and Marlborough in Wiltshire to Ivinghoe in Buckinghamshire. It was designated an official long-distance path by the Countryside Commission, which, together with the County Councils of the areas through which the route runs (Wiltshire, Oxfordshire, Berkshire, Buckinghamshire and Hertfordshire), has overall responsibility for the Path. Its route was opened at an official ceremony on Coombe Hill on 29 September 1973.

The Path was created to take advantage of the historical associations of the prehistoric trading route, known as the Great Ridgeway, and of the line of chalk hills which stretches across Wiltshire into Hertfordshire and forms the twin Areas of Outstanding Natural Beauty of the North Wessex Downs and the Chilterns. Compared with the South-West Peninsula Coast Path, the Cleveland Way or the Pennine Way, the scenery is not spectacular, but nobody with a sense of history can fail to be moved as they walk past so many reminders of our distant ancestors. For much of the way, the route follows a line of hills which is considerably higher than the land on either side and it is often possible to see for miles across the vales and plains.

From the start at Overton Hill, the Ridgeway Path climbs to the top of the Wiltshire Downs, and it remains on the top of the downs (except when it crosses the motorway and the valley formed by the river Og) until reaching the Thames at Streatley (mile 43). At this point the route leaves the ancient Ridgeway and follows the old Icknield Way at the base of the hills. At Princes Risborough (mile 70), the Path climbs to the top of the Chiltern Hills and runs through glorious beechwoods until, at Tring (mile 85), the chalk hills become bare again.

The whole of the route from Overton Hill to Streatley (mile 43) is open to both riders and cyclists. Unfortunately, parts of it may also be used by motor vehicles, and some trials riders delight in exhibiting their skill and shattering the peace of the countryside. Let us hope that the moves afoot to ban all motor vehicles (except farm vehicles) from the Ridgeway will be successful. Short stretches of the eastern half of the Path where it follows the Icknield Way are also bridleway, but it is impossible for riders and cyclists to complete the whole of the route.

Long-distance paths were established for pleasure, not for record-breaking purposes. Because our lives are governed by the need to conserve time, there is an unfortunate tendency to try to walk a route as quickly as possible. Unless you derive particular pleasure from testing yourself to the limit, take plenty of time and savour every moment of the walk. It is much better to be able to laze in the sun after a pleasant lunch, to explore some of the ancient monuments along the route, to watch the wildlife and examine the flowers than to have the nagging urge to keep going at all costs in order to meet a tight schedule. Those who have walked long-distance paths know what Robert Louis Stevenson meant when he wrote that 'To travel hopefully is a better thing than to arrive'.

As long-distance paths go, the Ridgeway is an easy walk. The significant hills are few, the gradients are rarely steep and it makes an ideal introduction to the pleasures of long-distance walking. It is particularly suitable for young people seeking their first taste of adventure. Although the Path passes through few towns, and on the first half there are scarcely any houses along the route, yet it is crossed frequently by roads and help is never far away. The worst hazard likely to be met is mud and, providing the advice about carrying plenty of water (see p. 11) is heeded, nobody should come to any harm.

Many people walk the Ridgeway Path in the course of a year and if its charm and beauty is to be preserved it is incumbent upon *everyone* to avoid polluting it and thus making it unpleasant for those who follow. Never on any account drop litter or light fires. All litter should be carried in a plastic bag until it can be deposited properly in a litter bin. Do not hide it behind a convenient bush – out of sight is not always out of mind, and hidden plastic bags may be swallowed by farm animals, or a favourite pony, possibly with fatal results. Tin cans can cause serious injuries to livestock. When nature calls, retire to some protective bushes, scrape a shallow pit with the heel of your boot, or with a stick, and cover the stools and toilet tissue with a sprinkling of soil. If all Britons would obey the instructions contained in the Country Code, which has been preached at them for many, many years, we would soon lose the reputation of having the dirtiest country in Europe.

Guard against all risk of fire
Fasten all gates
Keep dogs under proper control
Keep to the paths across farm land
Avoid damaging fences, walls and hedges
Leave no litter
Safeguard water supplies
Protect wild life, wild plants and trees
Go carefully on country roads
Respect the life of the countryside

Planning the walk

When planning a walk along any long-distance path the walker always has to make two decisions which will affect the course of all his actions. The first decision is in which direction to walk the Path. The second is whether to walk the Path in consecutive days or to make a series of single-day excursions. Direction is a matter of personal preference. Most people walk from west to east (Overton Hill to Ivinghoe), which means that they have the prevailing wind behind them. But there is much to be said for walking from east to west (Ivinghoe to Overton Hill), as the views are better and wayfarers with a sense of history will be walking towards the most exciting part of the route. Indeed, Avebury can be regarded as a goal for the modern pilgrim. Such is the heightened awareness which several days on foot will induce that you would not be surprised to hear, as you make the final descent along the Herepath, the sound of celebration from within the sacred confines of the stone circle, the blaring of trumpets from a great funeral procession at Wayland's Smithy, the measured tramp of a Roman legion marching from Londinium to Aquae Sulis, the despairing sounds of battle as King Arthur tries to hold off the Saxons at Barbury Castle and the whistling flight of an arrow from a nomadic hunter in search of food for his family.

Walkers who prefer to walk the Path in a series of separate day excursions will find this feasible with a little forethought. The twin towns of Goring and Streatley (mile 43) are the midway point and are about 50 miles from London and Southampton, 60 miles from Bristol and 80 miles from Birmingham.

The M4 runs parallel to the Path and is never more than a few miles away, the M40 crosses the Path near Watlington, the M5 serves the western end and the M1 is conveniently near the eastern terminus.

Public transport along the line of the Path is very poor and what services exist tend to cross the route rather than run parallel to it. A convenient method for two or more people to walk the Path over a period of time using only one car is for the party to divide into two groups. The first party is dropped off at the end of the second party's walk and the second party then drives to the beginning of their walk and the end of the first party's day. On reaching the car, the first party drives to pick up the second party. Two drivers and two sets of keys are required, and there must be no doubt where the car is to be left!

Unless it is possible to persuade a relative or friend to deliver and collect you from the termini of the Path, most walkers walking the route on consecutive days will find it more convenient to use public transport. Fortunately both Avebury and Ivinghoe are well served by bus and rail services. The best way to reach Avebury by public transport is to go by rail to Swindon and then to take the Bristol Omnibus service 471 (Swindon to Devizes), which passes through Avebury. Ivinghoe can be reached from Tring, on the main line from Euston to the midlands and the north-west (Tring station is actually on the Ridgeway Path), and then by United Counties service 561 from Aylesbury to Luton.

Accommodation

There is only a very limited amount of accommodation along the Ridgeway Path and some of it lies a mile or so off the route. Anyone planning to walk the Path using bed and breakfast establishments is advised to book in advance. Places where accommodation is available are mentioned in the text and there is a complete list, arranged in geographical order from west to east, on pp. 99–102. The author would be grateful for any suitable additions to the accommodation list for inclusion in future editions of this guide. Please write to him c/o Penguin Books Ltd, 536 King's Road, London SW10 0UH.

The only Youth Hostels along the route are at Streatley (mile 43), Bradenham (4 miles off the Path from mile 70 but with a good bus service), Lee Gate (1 mile off the Path at mile 79), and Ivinghoe. There are no convenient hostels serving the western half.

Two friends of mine once rented a holiday flat in Streatley and, using two cars, walked the length of the Ridgeway Path in consecutive days.

Many walkers take a tent and backpack along the Path. There are official camp sites near the route at Wallingford (mile 49), Chivery (mile 80) and near Ivinghoe. Properly speaking, one should never camp without first asking permission from the landowner, but many sections of the Path (especially the western half and where it follows the line of the Icknield Way) are so wide that it is possible to camp within the boundaries of the Path without causing any obstruction. Never, on any account, camp in fields or woods off the Path without permission. If you are discovered by a farmer or gamekeeper you will be turned off unceremoniously at what is likely to be a very inconvenient time.

Water

The biggest problem facing backpackers is the almost complete lack of water. The only legitimate sources of potable water are public houses, shops (assuming that you have patronized them and they are not too busy to fill your bottle) and public loos in some of the towns. In areas where animal husbandry is practised, cattle troughs may be found in fields adjacent to the Path. However, they may not be connected to a water supply and in any case there is no certainty that the water is drinkable. Mains water supplied to farms is metered and the farmer pays for what is consumed, so taking water from a cattle trough is justified only in a genuine emergency. Do not make a nuisance of yourself by asking for water at houses along the Path.

Clothing and equipment

No special clothing or equipment is required to walk this lowland Path. Except after long dry periods, mud is likely to be encountered and suitable footwear should be worn. Boots and canvas or nylon gaiters are best, but stout shoes will suffice. I have walked long sections of the Path in wellington boots and, contrary to received opinion, have suffered no ill-effects and have been perfectly comfortable, though I should not care to do it in very hot weather. For foul weather, a nylon raincoat and overtrousers, or a plastic or nylon suit (available from anglers' shops), are all that is needed. Obviously, if the purse extends far enough it is better to buy a cagoule, anorak or waterproof walking jacket. Avoid wearing jeans, as they are usually cut far too tight for comfort and are miserably cold when wet. Breeches, or an old pair of light worsted trousers tucked into long woollen socks, are much more satisfactory.

All walkers will require a rucksack suitable for their needs. Day walkers will have to carry food and drink and foul-weather gear. Never, on any account, rely for food and drink on public houses and cafés; they may be sold out when you arrive, or you may be delayed and arrive to find them closed. Those backpacking, bed-and-breakfasting or Youth Hostelling will require a rucksack large enough to contain all that they need. The weight of all equipment, kit and food carried in the rucksack should not exceed 30 lb. Backpackers can keep the weight down by sharing certain items of equipment, such as tents, cooking equipment and food.

How to use the guide

The purpose of this guide is to provide all the information that the walker requires to enable him to walk the route of the Ridgeway Path, either from the east or from the west. The main body of the guide comprises 33 strip maps of the route on a scale of 1:25000 (approximately $2\frac{1}{2}$ inches to the mile) which show the route in very great detail, including information such as the location of gates, stiles, signposts and way-marks which the Ordnance Survey do not show on their maps. In addition, although based on the Ordnance Survey maps (with the sanction of the Controller of Her Majesty's Stationery Office), they have been updated by means of personal survey and are thus more accurate.

A great deal of thought has gone into the design of the maps and they must be studied carefully in conjunction with the key in order to get the most from them. To reduce the amount of unnecessary detail and to avoid cluttering them unduly, contour and grid lines have been omitted. Instead, grid line numbers form the frame of each map, so that it is possible to relate them to any Ordnance Survey map and to use a compass, if required. Instead of indicating heights in the conventional way, a profile of the Path is shown in half scale at the bottom of every map. The numbers in the path profile relate to the mile numbers given on the map. In this way it is possible to see at a glance whether the section of the route to be walked is easy or strenuous.

It has already been said that the guide can be used in either direction. North, although always indicated, is of academic interest only and is not always at the top of the page. The guide is designed to be held in a natural reading position in front of the walker. Those travelling eastward towards Ivinghoe start at the front of the guide and their eyes follow the route *up* the page. Wayfarers travelling westward, towards Overton Hill, start at the back of the guide and their eyes go *down* the page. The only disadvantage that those travelling west will be under is that the text will have to be read in reverse order (paragraph by paragraph, *not* word by word!).

Opposite every map is the relevant section of text. Here will be found brief notes of interesting things to be seen along the way and, wherever route finding is difficult, a description of the route to supplement the map. Information given in the text includes the location of shops, banks, post offices, cafés, restaurants, public houses and accommodation. Early closing days are given together with brief details of the availability of public transport.

Great care has been taken in the compilation of this guide but wayfarers should be aware that the countryside is constantly changing and that time may render parts of this guide out of date. In particular, vandals may vent their wrath on waymarks and signposts. The author would be most grateful for comments and criticisms as well as information about changes which have made the guide out of date. Please write c/o Penguin Books Ltd, 536 King's Road, London SW10 0UH. Neither the author nor the publisher can accept any responsibility for the consequences incurred if the wayfarer departs from the right of way.

The guide is intended to be complete in itself and to contain everything that the wayfarer needs to know. However, some walkers like to have a general map which will place the route in the general context of the surrounding countryside. If the map on p. 30 does not contain sufficient detail the reader is recommended to buy one of the motoring maps published by several of the oil companies. On many of them the western half of the Ridgeway Path is shown and it takes but a few minutes to mark in the rest of the route. This is easily the cheapest way of obtaining a general map.

The Story of the Ridgeway Path

A brief examination of the two 1:50000 Ordnance Survey maps which cover the area between Overton Hill and the Thames at Streatley (sheets 173 and 174) will give an indication of the vast number of barrows, tumuli, hill forts, ancient trackways and other prehistoric remains which lie close to or actually on the line of the Ridgeway Path. In the course of the first 40 miles or so, the walker will pass like a traveller in time through many thousands of years of history. Those who have some knowledge and understanding of the significance of the prehistoric remains to be seen along the route will derive that much more enjoyment from their walk, and the account of the history of the Path which follows should provide enough basic information to set the subject in its historical context. Though not written by an expert, it is a summary of our present knowledge and few archaeologists would dissent significantly from it. Those interested in fringe archaeology and earth mysteries will be disappointed. Prehistoric man probably looked at the world in a different way from us and some of his monuments may have a significance that escapes us, but the evidence put forward by those who believe in, for instance, ley lines and psychic archaeology seems to me unconvincing.

Archaeologists have been able to tell us a great deal about our prehistoric forbears from the excavations they have made, but most of them would admit that there is one great gap in our knowledge that we are never likely to fill. Writing was unknown in this country until introduced by the Romans and so we know nothing of the religious beliefs and little of the social organization of the builders of these monuments. The best that we can do is to make some intelligent guesses. For example, it is reasonable to infer that a structure as enormous as Avebury, which clearly must have imposed a strain on the available workforce, had some considerable religious or ceremonial importance. Again, we know nothing of these beliefs, but from what we know of primitive religions throughout the world it is possible to guess that they worshipped some

15

form of fertility god such as the sun or the Great Earth Mother.

It is not too difficult for modern man to put himself in the position of a neolithic farmer. Imagine that you can calculate and predict the seasons and the rising and the setting of the sun. Since you have no knowledge of the scientific principles which account for these phenomena and as our English weather is wayward, there must always be a lurking fear at the back of your mind that one year the spring would not come or that flash flood or drought would wipe out the crops and your family would starve. Even modern farmers occasionally have to face disasters on a national scale. It is not so many years ago that foot-and-mouth disease nearly destroyed all the cattle in this country. Farmers suffered, though they were cushioned to some extent by government compensation, but the general public did not, because the shortfall in milk and beef could be made up from imports. Such remedies were not open to the neolithic farmer. Imagine him then, lying on a bed of straw in a small mud-walled thatched hut listening to the gentle sounds of sleep from his family, wife, children and aged parents. The spring is cold and the corn has not yet germinated. Outside in the woods beyond the fields the wolves are howling. 'Great Earth Mother, warm the soil so that the corn will grow and my children will not die!' The desire to placate the anger of the gods is a basic human instinct the whole world over. Many a city-dwelling backpacker, unused to the sounds of the countryside, has been frightened out of his wits while lying in his tent by the unearthly scream of a vixen. Fear is never far below the surface of the human mind.

In order to understand what the prehistoric landscape was like we must appreciate what man has done to the environment during the course of countless centuries. The most significant change is probably not the most obvious. The first difference that neolithic man would notice is the clearance of the forest, but what has turned southern England into fertile farmland is the complicated drainage system. The Thames and its tributaries have been channelled and contained by a system of locks, sluices, dykes and barrages so that it is now a comparatively narrow, deep and steadily flowing river. The surface water that falls on the fields is drawn into ditches and gulleys and ultimately to the river and the sea by an underground system of field drains. Our early farmer would be astonished at the *lack* of water in southern England, for although we still get more than our fair share of rain, the surplus water which the soil cannot absorb is quickly and efficiently returned to the sea whence it came.

Let us now go back some 8,000 years in time before man had had any effect on the primeval forest which covered the country. It was about this time that the sea broke through the narrow isthmus which still connected England to Europe and we became an island. The rivers were wide and meandered from one side of the valley to the other through marshes and bogs, and forests clothed the hillsides. It was extremely difficult to move about except on the top of the chalk hills, where, because the soil was poor, the forest tended to be less dense. Agriculture had not yet been introduced into Europe and the population consisted of nomadic hunters and fishers who eked out a pretty miserable existence. It is likely that herds of animals such as deer and wild pigs made game paths through the forest between their grazing grounds and watering places and that early man who preyed on them used these paths too. Longer paths were made by migrating animals and early man followed these too, for his very existence depended upon being able to prey upon the game.

Trading routes were probably established along the tops of the chalk hills, using the paths which the hunters and the animals had made, and it is likely that one of these routes was the one we now know as the Ridgeway Path, which ultimately ran from Axmouth in east Devon to the Wash, utilizing for most of the way the line of low chalk hills.

In about 3000 BC the first farmers arrived in Britain. It is interesting to speculate why they risked their lives by crossing the English Channel. One theory is that fishermen were blown out to sea, made a landfall and liked what they found. Another suggests that although these people practised farming, they had no knowledge of crop rotation and the nitrogen cycle and so they soon exhausted the soil and had to move on. Ultimately they reached the northern coast of France and, seeing England on the other side of the sea, made the voyage in search of new and fertile lands.

These first farmers used flint tools and left behind them significant remains. A little to the west of the Ridgeway and just to the north of Avebury is the causewayed camp of Windmill Hill, which has given its name to this particular culture. About fifteen other causewayed camps are known in southern England and many more have probably been destroyed by ploughing. The camp on Windmill Hill consists of three concentric rings of earthworks and has been dated, using the radio carbon technique, to about 2750 BC. It is not a defensive fort but an enclosure for sheltering cattle, the inhabitants living outside in thatched huts.

The Windmill Hill people buried their important dead in massive long barrows of which the two most famous examples are at West Kennett, just south of Overton Hill, and Wayland's Smithy, which is actually on the Ridgeway. They are massive structures containing chambered tombs made from stones and heaped up with earth, and one can only assume that those buried in them were of special significance to the community and were either royalty or priests. They also built Silbury Hill, an artificial mound 130 ft high, covering $5\frac{1}{2}$ acres and surrounded by a ditch 125 ft wide and 30 ft deep, and Avebury.

The Windmill Hill people practised farming and cleared enclaves by slashing with stone axes and burning. Later pigs were turned loose and in this way the forest was cleared. The flint they required for making tools was obtained from Brandon in Norfolk, where there are extensive flint mines in which have been found antler picks, oil lamps and a shrine to a goddess. The Ridgeway was almost certainly used as a trading route for these goods.

The next great event in our history was the introduction of metal tools made of bronze. These were brought in by the Beaker people who started to arrive on these shores from the Rhine delta in about 2400 BC. They derive their name from the characteristic shape of their pottery. They were a remarkable people and achieved a very high level of social organization. Avebury, the largest stone circle in Britain, was used by them, and they set about enlarging Stonehenge by transporting the bluestones, weighing some 40 tons each, from Pembrokeshire.

The next wave of settlers, who came into Britain in about 700 BC, brought with them iron. Bronze, which was used by the Beaker people, was quite difficult to make, as it is an alloy of copper and tin and the known deposits were becoming depleted. Iron, on the other hand, was not only more plentiful but was also easier to work and the tools made from it were of better quality. The Iron Age settlers lived in farms and small villages. They kept cattle, sheep and pigs and grew corn, which was stored in underground granaries. Sheep require more open pasture than does arable farming, which means that there must have been considerable clearance of the forest and scrub. By now the downland landscape was probably not too different from what it is like now except that it was not under the plough.

It was around 500 BC that many of the Iron Age hill forts were built. Those at Barbury Castle, Liddington Castle, Uffington Castle and Letcombe Castle lie on or very close to the Ridgeway, are very large and appear to have been built to defend the upper Thames valley. All of them lie above the spring line and it is believed that either the water table must have been higher or that dew ponds were constructed to provide drinking water.

In AD 43, one of the most significant events in the history of these islands occurred when the Romans landed in Kent and within five years had occupied and colonized most of southern England from Dorset to the Wolds. There are many points of similarity between the Roman and British attitudes to their respective empires. The Romans had a genius for warfare, engineering and civil administration. Having defeated the British tribes they built an excellent road system which they required for quick communication and for the rapid deployment of troops. The Roman army was composed of an heterogeneous collection of tribes and nationalities all owing allegiance to their cohort, eagle and ultimately to Caesar. It was superbly disciplined and virtually invincible. Having conquered a territory and secured its frontiers, the Romans were quite content to allow the population to continue its way of life provided that this posed no threat to the Pax Romana. Native gods and the indigenous culture were tolerated, but the Roman way of life was so attractive, as the standard of living was high, that the native aristocracy quickly adopted the ways of their conquerors and soon became thoroughly Romanized.

It is doubtful if the Romans used the Ridgeway to any great extent. They may have done so during the time that they were campaigning, but it was not the sort of road to appeal to them and they soon built their own roads which connected their settlements in the Thames valley. The forts probably fell into disuse during the Roman occupation, but when the Saxon invasion took place after the withdrawal of Roman troops, the Romano-British forces used them to guard the valley, and we know that an important battle against the invading Saxons took place at Barbury Castle in AD 556.

During the ninth century the Ridgeway was an important line of defence against the Danes, who were attempting to push south from the Thames. King Alfred defeated the Danes at the Battle of Edington (878).

During the medieval period the importance of the Ridgeway as a through route declined and until the coming of the turn-pikes in the eighteenth century it remained of local importance only. It was the custom to supply London with fresh meat by driving cattle and sheep from as far away as Wales and Scot-land for slaughter at Smithfield. For centuries the drovers had followed the main roads, but the tolls levied on the turnpikes made this very expensive and the droving trade took to the byways, the Ridgeway being used as part of the link in the chain from Wales. The coming of the railways killed droving within a very short time.

And so the Ridgeway fell into disuse again until rediscovered by modern travellers as a recreational route.

The Icknield Way

The modern long-distance Ridgeway Path follows the line of the ancient trackway, except for a short diversion along Smeathe's Ridge, from Overton Hill to Streatley. From Streatley to Ivinghoe it is a modern creation, although it follows for considerable stretches another ancient trackway known as the Icknield Way. The origin of its name is not known for certain; it may be connected with the Iceni, the warlike tribe of East Anglia, or derive from the Old English for oxen.

It runs from Wells-next-the-Sea in Norfolk via Swaffham, Newmarket, Royston, Luton, Dunstable, Ivinghoe, Wendover, Chinnor, Watlington and Goring, where it links with the Ridgeway. For much of its length it has been incorporated into the modern road system, but parts of it still survive as a green lane. In places there are parallel routes given distinguishing names such as the Upper and Lower Icknield Way and it is believed that this is a relic of the time when roads were so poor that it was useful to have a winter route which kept to higher ground and a summer route which was faster when the ground was firm.

Geology

The chalk hills which the Ridgeway follows were laid down in the Cretaceous periods of the Mesozoic era, which in places has been overlaid with deposits of gravels and clay with flints. The only significant variation from this pattern is in the Thames valley, which is made up of gault and Kimmeridge and Oxford clays. There are a number of gaps in the chalk ridge which have been cut by streams, most of which have long since disappeared.

Fauna and Flora

It is probable that for many thousands of years from neolithic times the downland over which the Ridgeway Path crosses was grazed by sheep, and it was only in the eighteenth century that the ancient turf was ploughed. Greensward which has been grown under such conditions does not produce flowers because the sheep crop the grass to a height of about two inches. Instead, shoots appear at the base of the plant which intertwine with each other to form a very dense springy turf. Grasses which make up this kind of turf include red fescue and sheep's fescue.

Traditional plants of the downland chalk include salad burnet, small scabious, stemless thistle, fairy flax, hairy hawkbit, ribwort plantain, bird's foot trefoil, restharrow, melilot, eyebright, dropwort, greater knapweed and the pyramidal orchid. Rarer species which may be found by the keen naturalist include the musk orchid, the frog orchid, the Chiltern gentian and field fleawort.

The species of butterflies which love the chalk include the chalk hill blue, the small heath brown, the gate keeper, wall brown and ringlet brown, but most varieties have suffered as a result of the postwar use of pesticides.

Among the birds, raptors are not very common, but ornithologists may spot the occasional buzzard, hobby and peregrine falcon and the much more rare Montague's harrier and marsh harrier. On the Thames it is possible to see kingfishers, crested and little grebes, mallard, coot, moorhen and Canada geese. Rarer species which the fortunate may be able to observe include the cirl bunting, stone curlew and quail.

In the Chilterns there are splendid groves of beechwoods and near Chequers is one of the finest stands of boxwood in England.

Badgers and foxes are plentiful, although the former is unlikely to be seen, and both fallow deer and the muntjac or chinese barking deer haunt the wooded thickets along the Path.

Book List

Ridgeway guides

Burden, Vera, *Discovering the Ridgeway*, 2nd edn, Shire
    Publications, 1978.
Cull, Elizabeth, *Walks along the Ridgeway*, Spurbooks, 1977.
Jennett, Sean, *The Ridgeway Path*, H M S O, 1976.
Westacott, H. D., *A Practical Guide to Walking the Ridgeway
    Path*, 4th edn, Footpath Publications, 1978.

Geology

Sherlock, R. L., *London and the Thames Valley*, H M S O,
    1971.

Archaeology

Atkinson, R. J. C., *Stonehenge and Avebury*, revised edn,
    H M S O, 1972.
Bord, Janet, and Bord, Colin, *A Guide to Ancient Sites in
    Britain*, Latimer, 1978.
Clayton, Peter, *Archaeological Sites of Britain*, Weidenfeld &
    Nicolson, 1976.
Cunliffe, Barry, *Iron Age Communities in Britain*, 2nd edn,
    Routledge & Kegan Paul, 1978.
Dames, Michael, *The Silbury Treasure*, Thames & Hudson,
    1976.
Daniel, Glyn, *The Megalith Builders of Western Europe*,
    Penguin Books, 1962.
Dyer, James, *Southern England: An Archaeological Guide*,
    Faber, 1973.
Fowler, P. J., Wessex: *A Regional Archaeology*, Heinemann,
    1967.
Harrison, Richard J., *The Beaker Folk*, Thames & Hudson,
    1980.
Hogg, A. H. A., *Hill-Forts of Britain*, Hart-Davis, MacGibbon,
    1975.
Laing, Lloyd, *Celtic Britain*, Routledge & Kegan Paul, 1979.

Marples, Morris, *White Horses and Other Hill Figures*, Country Life, 1970.

Ordnance Survey, Ancient Britain, south sheet: A map of the major visible antiquities of Great Britain before 1066, 2nd edn, Ordnance Survey, 1964.

Piggott, Stuart, *The West Kennett Long Barrow*, H M S O, 1971.

Powell, T. G. F., *The Celts*, 2nd edn, Thames & Hudson, 1980.

Smith, Isobel, *Windmill Hill and Avebury*, Oxford University Press, 1965.

Thom, Alexander, *Megalithic Sites in Britain*, Oxford University Press, 1967.

Wainwright, Richard, *A Guide to the Prehistoric Remains in Britain*, Vol. 1, South and East, Constable, 1978.

Wood, Eric S., *Collins' Field Guide to Archaeology in Britain*, 5th edn, Collins, 1979.

History

Anderson, J. R. L., and Godwin, Fay, *The Oldest Road: An Exploration of the Ridgeway*, Wildwood House, 1975.

Bulfield, Anthony, *The Icknield Way*, Dalton, 1972.

Cox, R. Hippisley, *The Green Roads of England* (1914), Garnstone, 1973.

Taylor, Christopher, *Roads and Tracks of Britain*, Dent, 1979.

Thomas, Edward, *The Icknield Way* (1913), Wildwood House, 1980.

Timperley, H. W., and Brill, Edith, *Ancient Trackways of Wessex*, Phoenix House, 1965.

Natural history

Jefferies, Richard, *The Story of My Heart* (1883), Quartet Books, 1979.

Jefferies, Richard, *Wildlife in a Southern County* (1879), Moonraker, 1978.

Wiltshire

Hammond, Reginald J. W., *Complete Dorset and Wiltshire*, Ward, Lock, 1976.

Mee, Arthur, *Wiltshire*, Hodder & Stoughton, 1939.

Book List

Pevsner, Nikolaus, *Buildings of England: Wiltshire*, 2nd edn,
    Penguin Books, 1975.
Street, Pamela, *Portrait of Wiltshire*, Hale, 1971.
Whitlock, Ralph, *Wiltshire*, Batsford, 1976.

Berkshire

Beckinsale, R. P., *Companion into Berkshire*, 2nd edn,
    Spurbooks, 1972.
Hammond, Nigel, *The White Horse Country: A Berkshire Book*,
    William Smith Ltd, 1972.
Higham, Roger, *Berkshire and the Vale of the White Horse*,
    Batsford, 1977.
Mee, Arthur, *Berkshire*, 2nd edn, Hodder & Stoughton, 1964.
Pevsner, Nikolaus, *Buildings of England: Berkshire*, Penguin
    Books, 1966.
Yarrow, Ian, *Berkshire*, 2nd edn, Hale, 1974.

The Chilterns

Bailey, Brian J., *View of the Chilterns*, Hale, 1979.
Burden, Vera, *Chiltern Villages: History, People, Places in the
    Chiltern Hills*, Spurbooks, 1972.
Crosher, G. R., *Along the Chiltern Ways*, Cassell, 1973.
Dickson, Annan, *Portrait of the Chiltern Hills*, Hale, 1951.
Fitzgerald, Kevin, *The Chilterns*, Batsford, 1972.
Hay, David, *Hill Top Villages of the Chilterns*, Phillimore,
    1971.
Peel, J. H. B., *The Chilterns*, Elek, 1950.

Oxfordshire (see also under Chilterns)

Martin, Frank, *History, People and Places in the New
    Oxfordshire*, Spurbooks, 1975.
Mee, Arthur, *Oxfordshire*, 2nd edn, Hodder & Stoughton,
    1965.
Pevsner, Nikolaus, *The Buildings of England: Oxfordshire*,
    Penguin Books, 1974.

Buckinghamshire (see also under Chilterns)

Camp, John, *Portrait of Buckinghamshire*, Hale, 1972.
Fraser, Maxwell, *Companion into Buckinghamshire* (1950),
    Spurbooks, 1972.

Mee, Arthur, *Buckinghamshire*, 2nd edn, Hodder & Stoughton, 1965.

Pevsner, Nikolaus, *Buildings of England: Buckinghamshire*, Penguin Books, 1960.

Hertfordshire (see also under Chilterns)

Bailey, Brian John, *Portrait of Hertfordshire*, Hale, 1978.

Meadows, Eric George, *Hertfordshire: A Pictorial Guide*, White Crescent Press, 1979.

Mee, Arthur, *Hertfordshire*, 2nd edn, Hodder & Stoughton, 1965.

Pevsner, Nikolaus, *Buildings of England: Hertfordshire*, 2nd edn, Penguin Books, 1977.

Guide and Sectional Maps

The Ridgeway Path

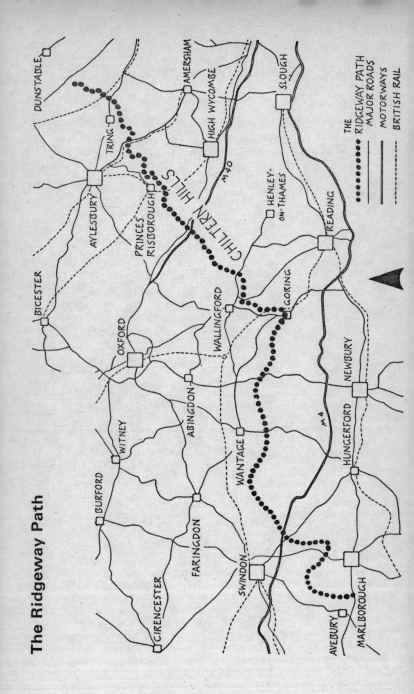

THE
RIDGEWAY PATH
MAJOR ROADS
MOTORWAYS
BRITISH RAIL

DUNSTABLE

TRING

AYLESBURY

PRINCES
RISBOROUGH

AMERSHAM

HIGH WYCOMBE

M 40

SLOUGH

CHILTERN HILLS

HENLEY-
ON-THAMES

READING

BICESTER

OXFORD

WALLINGFORD

GORING

NEWBURY

ABINGDON

M 4

HUNGERFORD

WITNEY

WANTAGE

BURFORD

SWINDON

MARLBOROUGH

FARINGDON

AVEBURY

CIRENCESTER

KEY

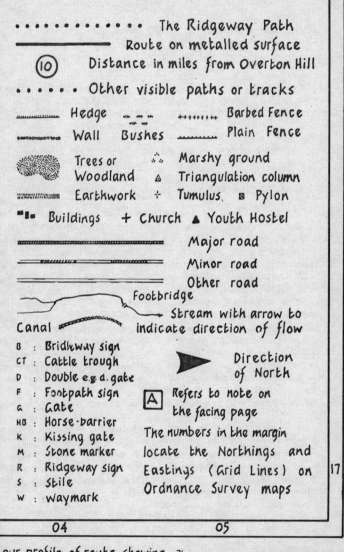

· · · · · · · · · · · · ·   The Ridgeway Path

————————   Route on metalled surface

⑩   Distance in miles from Overton Hill

· · · · · ·   Other visible paths or tracks

‗‗‗‗‗‗   Hedge   ‑ ‑ ‑   ┼┼┼┼┼┼┼   Barbed Fence

⌐∘∘∘∘∘⌐   Wall   Bushes   ‗‗‗‗‗‗   Plain Fence

Trees or Woodland   ˙ˑ˙   Marshy ground

△   Triangulation column

Earthwork   ÷   Tumulus   ⊠   Pylon

▀▪▐   Buildings   ✛ Church   ▲ Youth Hostel

▓▓▓▓▓▓▓▓   Major road

▭▭▭   Minor road

————————   Other road

Footbridge

Canal   Stream with arrow to indicate direction of flow

B : Bridleway sign
CT : Cattle trough
D : Double e.g. d. gate
F : Footpath sign
G : Gate
HB : Horse-barrier
K : Kissing gate
M : Stone marker
R : Ridgeway sign
S : Stile
W : Waymark

►   Direction of North

Ⓐ Refers to note on the facing page

The numbers in the margin locate the Northings and Eastings (Grid Lines) on Ordnance Survey maps

17   17

04   05

Contour profile of route showing Milepoints and height in metres   76 ---------   30 ----   10

31

1. Overton Hill, Avebury Down

1½ miles
Maps: 1:25000 sheet SU16; 1:50000 sheet 173

The official start of the Ridgeway Path is Overton Hill, a few yards to the east of the Ridgeway Café on the A4, which serves hearty meals for long-distance lorry drivers as well as for long-distance walkers. There is a large car park for the use of those eating at the café, *but do not park here for longer than the duration of your meal.* There is a lay-by a short distance along the road towards Marlborough.

Just to the south of the A4 lies the site known as the Sanctuary, a small timber and stone circle which was excavated in 1930.

Many walkers will want to visit the attractive village of Avebury before starting their long march. It has an interesting church and a folk museum, but it is most famous for its stone circle and the near-by artificial Silbury Hill. The stone circle is a massive structure enclosing nearly 30 acres with a ditch that is 30 ft deep and a bank surmounted by 98 sarsen stones weighing up to 40 tons each. It was probably built by the Windmill Hill people (see p. 18) in about 2600 B C. Such an enterprise must have had enormous religious significance and the proximity to Silbury Hill and the West Kennett long barrow must have made Avebury an important centre of prehistoric life.

Silbury Hill was also built by the Windmill Hill people and has been dated to about 2750 B C. It is 130 ft high, covers 5½ acres and is surrounded by a ditch 125 ft wide and 30 ft deep. It has been excavated on a number of occasions and although we know how it is constructed we do not know what its significance is. It contains no grave nor was there ever a building on the top. One suggestion is that it represents the figure of the Earth Mother in the squatting or birth position. This possibility is strengthened by the fact that a spring issues from the side of the hill which floods at certain times of the year and some believe that this represents menstruation.

In Avebury, near the church, is a most interesting museum which explains in considerable detail what has been discovered on the sites in the immediate vicinity.

Avebury has a public house and bus services to Swindon and Devizes.

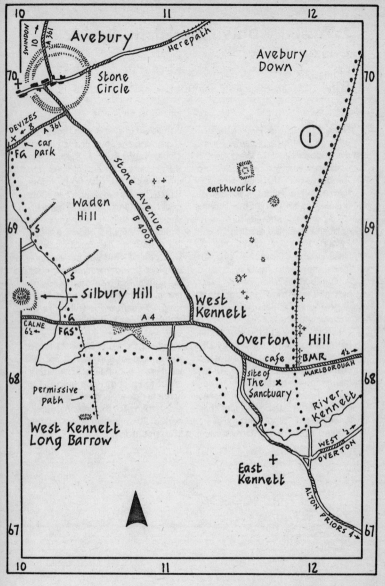

10   11   12

SWINDON 10 → A 361

Avebury

Herepath

Avebury Down

70   Stone Circle   70

DEVIZES × 8 ← A 361

FA car park

①

Stone Avenue B 4003

Waden Hill

earthworks

69   S   69

S

Silbury Hill

West Kennett

A 4

CALNE 6½ ←   FAS

Overton Hill

cafe   BMR   4½ →

MARLBOROUGH

68   site of The Sanctuary ×   68

permissive path →

River Kennett

WEST ½ OVERTON

West Kennett Long Barrow

East Kennett +

ALTON PRIORS 4 →

67   67

10   11   12

213 ·······
168

2. Avebury Down, Herepath, Berwick Bassett Down

$2\frac{1}{2}$ miles
Maps: 1:25000 sheets SUI6 and SU17; 1:50000 sheet 173

Near mile 2, the Herepath, another ancient trackway, crosses the Ridgeway Path. West-bound walkers wishing to go directly to Avebury (with its ancient monuments and museum – see previous page – and direct bus service to Swindon) should turn right opposite the gate leading to the Fyfield Down National Nature Reserve and follow the Herepath for $1\frac{1}{2}$ miles into Avebury.

'Herepath' is from the Old English and means a path or track wide enough to accommodate an army or multitude.

Fyfield Down, to the east of the path, is a large tract of well-preserved ancient landscape probably 4,000 years old. It remains in its primeval state because the large quantity of stones which litter the surface has discouraged ploughing. Nevertheless, parts of the Down were cultivated in prehistoric times and there are the remains of many Celtic field systems. Presumably these early farmers cleared the stones from the ground by hand. One of the sarsen stones has some curious cuts in it and it has been suggested that it was used for sharpening tools and weapons.

In 1965 an experimental barrow was constructed so that archaeologists could measure changes brought about by erosion and soil creep. Although it is now more than 15 years old it still looks as though it was constructed yesterday.

Fyfield Down is believed to be the source of the sarsen stones used in the building of Avebury and Stonehenge. The stones for Stonehenge, some weighing more than 40 tons, were transported 20 miles on rollers made from tree trunks.

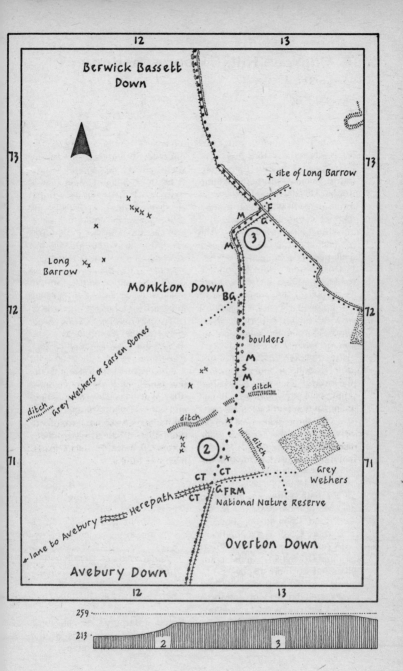

Berwick Bassett Down

73

site of Long Barrow

F

M

G

③

M

Long Barrow

Monkton Down

BG

boulders

M
S
M
S
ditch

ditch

Grey Wethers or Sarsen Stones

ditch

②

Grey Wethers

CT CT

CT FRM

National Nature Reserve

Herepath

lane to Avebury

Overton Down

Avebury Down

72

71

73

72

71

12

13

259
213

2

3

3. Hackpen Hill, Barbury Castle

2½ miles
Maps: 1:25000 sheet SU17; 1:50000 sheet 173

At mile 6 the modern Ridgeway Path leaves the historic line of the ancient trackway to follow another ancient route, Smeathe's Ridge. This diversion from the old route is made necessary because part of it has been incorporated into the modern road system. The original route is rejoined at Fox Hill, near mile 17.

On Hackpen Hill, though not visible from the Ridgeway Path, is a copy of the White Horse of Uffington cut into the hillside. It was made in 1838. 'Hackpen' is derived from the Old English *haca*, a hook, and *pen*, a hill.

At Barbury Castle, two 'unofficial' long-distance paths cross the Ridgeway. The Thamesdown Trail (path A7) is a 54-mile circular route around Swindon, and the Wiltshire Way (path A10) runs for 162 miles in a huge circle around Salisbury. (Both routes were devised by Laurence Main, who has written guides to them with the same title as the name of the paths. They are published by the Thornhill Press, 24 Moorend Road, Cheltenham, Glos.)

Barbury Castle is a magnificent Iron Age hill fort standing 880 ft on the Downs in a most commanding position. It covers 11½ acres and has two ramparts and associated ditches with entrances on the east and west. Excavations have revealed jewellery and chariot fittings and the existence of huts and storage pits inside the enclosure. Barbury Castle was probably refortified in the fifth or sixth century AD by the Britons after the Romans had left and it was used for defending the upper Thames valley against the Saxons. A great battle took place on the slopes below the hill fort in AD 556 when the Saxons defeated the Britons. The battle is recorded in the *Anglo-Saxon Chronicle* and given the name of the battle of Bera Byrg (which means Bera's hill – and it is possible that this records the name of the British Saxon leader, from which the name Barbury comes).

A large sarsen stone brought from Overton Down commemorate two local writers who loved the Wiltshire Downs. Richard Jefferies is acknowledged as one of Britain's greatest nature writers but Alfred Williams is scarcely known outside his native Wiltshire. The plaques read:

Richard Jefferies 1848–1887
It is eternity now
I am in the midst
of it. It is about
me in the sunshine.

Alfred Williams 1877–1930
Still to find and still to follow
Joy in every hill and hollow,
Company in solitude.

South of Barbury Castle are some earthworks, the remains of the deserted village of Barbury.

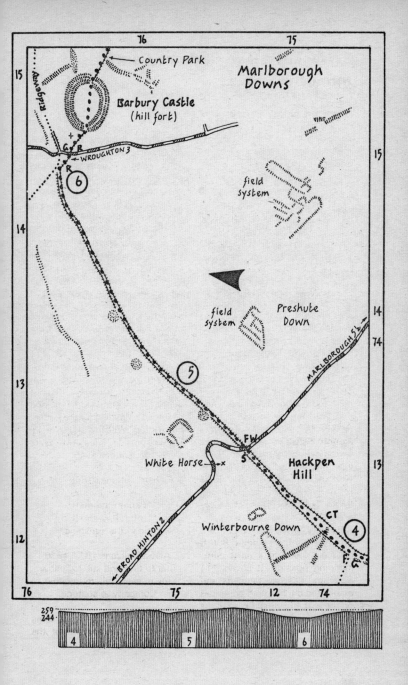

Marlborough Downs

Country Park

Barbury Castle
(hill fort)

Ridgeway

WROUGHTON 3

⑥

field
system

field
system

Preshute
Down

⑤

MARLBOROUGH 5½

FW

White Horse

S

Hackpen
Hill

CT

④

Winterbourne Down

BROAD HINTON 2

259
244

④   ⑤   ⑥

4. Barbury Down, Smeathe's Ridge, Ogbourne Down

2 miles
Maps: 1:25000 sheet SU17; 1:50000 sheet 174

At point A walkers travelling east must keep to the right of the information hut in the Barbury Castle Country Park. It is well worth visiting the information hut, where there is display material giving facts about Barbury Castle. There is also a map of the North Wessex Downs, posters illustrating some of the wildlife to be seen and brief accounts of Richard Jefferies, the nineteenth-century naturalist who greatly loved these downs, and of Alfred Williams, the Wiltshire nature poet. The Country Park has been created by the Wiltshire County Council.

Smeathe's (a variant of Smith) is a chalk ridge 690 ft high. Much of it is now under the plough.

Just before reaching the road, the Path passes the unsightly remains of an old military camp.

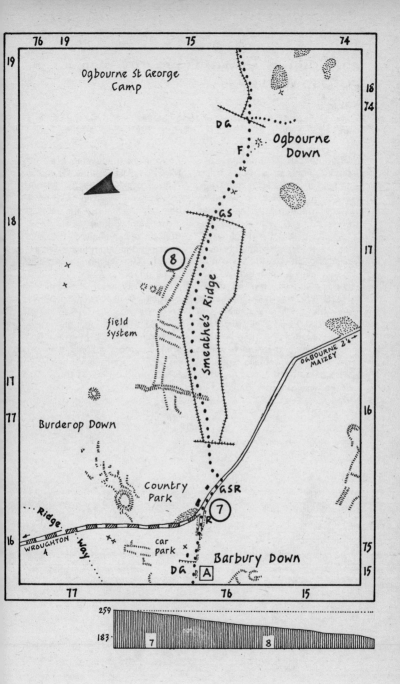

Ogbourne St George Camp

76 19   75   74

19   18
                                                                74
                                    DG
                                         F   Ogbourne
                                                    Down
18   17
                                    GS
              ⑧
                                    Smeathe's Ridge
     field
     system
                                                    Ogbourne 2¼
                                                    MAIZEY
17   16
77
     Burderop Down
                                                    GSR
                         Country
                         Park   ⑦
     Ridge
16   WROUGHTON   car park   75
           Way   Barbury Down
                         DG   Ⓐ
                                                                15
77   76   15

259
183   7   8

39

5. Coombe Down, Ogbourne St George, Chase Woods

3¼ miles
Maps: 1:25000 sheets SU17 and SU27; 1:50000 sheets 173 and 174

Ogbourne St George has two public houses, a post office stores, a café, accommodation and a bus service to Swindon, Marlborough and Savernake Forest.

It is a pleasant, straggling village with a parish church dedicated to St George, which is mainly Early English but has Perpendicular windows and tower. In 1873 it was heavily restored and the pitch-pine pews date from this period. The porch has both a sundial and a scratch dial. At the east end of the nave are the brasses of Thomas Goddard, who died in 1517, and his wife. There was once a Benedictine Priory here, founded in 1149 by Maud of Wallingford. The site is now occupied by the Manor House, with the date 1619 on a chimney stack.

The name Ogbourne is derived from the personal name Occa and *burna*, a stream – hence Occa's stream. Two villages took their name from the little river and are now distinguished by the patronal saints of their parish churches.

Walkers should take great care when crossing the busy A345 – after walking for some time on paths, it is frighteningly easy to forget how fast traffic travels on main roads.

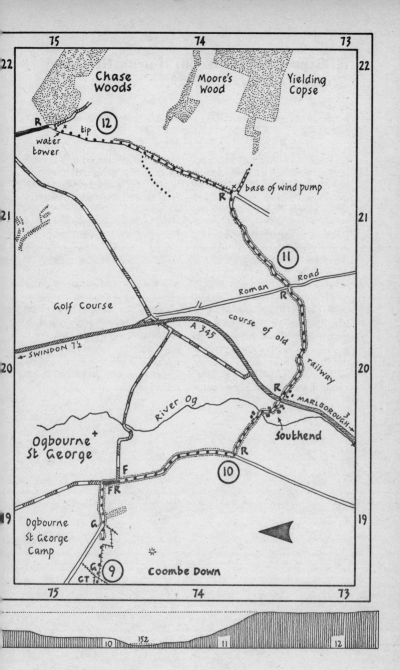

Chase Woods

Moore's Wood

Yielding Copse

R ×× tip ⑫
water tower

base of wind pump
R ×

⑪

Roman Road
R

Golf Course

A 345

course of old

← SWINDON 7½

railway

R MARLBOROUGH 3 →

River Og

Southend

Ogbourne St George +

R

F
FR ⑩

19

Ogbourne St George Camp

G.

⁎

G. ⑨
CT

Coombe Down

152 10   11   12

41

6. Round Hill Downs, Herepath

$2\frac{1}{2}$ miles
Maps: 1:25000 sheet SU27; 1:50000 sheet 173

Snap, $\frac{3}{4}$ mile to the east of the Path, is a deserted village. Its odd name is derived from the Old English *snaep* and means a boggy place which, as it lies in a bottom on the downs, is very appropriate. Snap is unusual in that it was abandoned not in medieval times but deliberately in the nineteenth century to make way for sheep. There was a theory that the Wiltshire Downs could be turned into vast sheep ranges, like those in Australia, watched over by a very few shepherds. The village was finally destroyed in 1913. It is ironic that sheep are now rare on the downs and have been superseded by cattle and cereals.

There are a number of villages which have been abandoned in comparatively recent times. Pertwood, in Wiltshire, was, like Snap, abandoned in favour of sheep, but most recent examples are the result of military activity. Imber, Wiltshire, and Tyneham, Dorset, are now part of army training grounds and access to them is severely restricted.

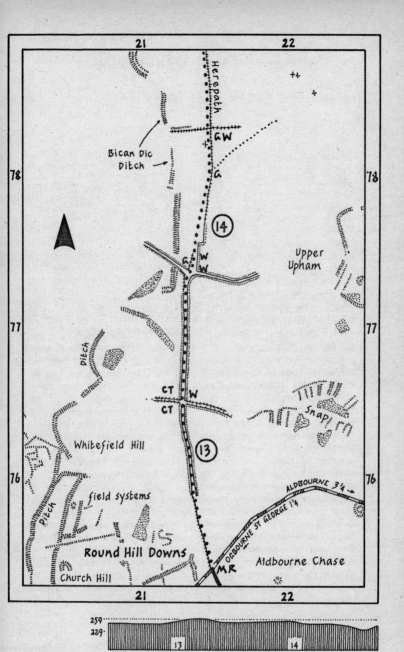

21   22

Herepath

GW

Bican Dic
Ditch

G

78   78

(14)

Upper
Upham

G   W
    W

77   77

Ditch

CT   W

CT

Snap

(13)

Whitefield Hill

76   76

ALDBOURNE 3¼ →

field systems

OGBOURNE ST GEORGE 1¼ →

Ditch

Round Hill Downs

Aldbourne Chase

Church Hill

MR

21   22

259
229

13   14

7. Liddington Castle, M4, Foxhill

3 miles
Maps: 1:25000 sheets SU27 and SU28; 1:50000 sheet 174

In a little over two miles the walker passes an Iron Age hill fort, crosses a modern motorway and a Roman road, and rejoins the ancient Ridgeway Path, which may be 8,000 years old.

Liddington (1 mile off the Path) has a public house, a post office and accommodation.

The parish church of All Saints dates from the thirteenth century but it was heavily restored in the 1880s. It has a Norman font. The near-by Manor House is Elizabethan and was originally moated. Part of it still remains.

Liddington Castle (sometimes known as Badbury Castle) is an oval Iron Age hill fort, just off the Path, covering 7½ acres and defended by a single rampart, faced with sarsen stones, and a ditch. The entrance is on the south-east side. There are a number of banks and ditches stretching for over 2 miles to the south which probably represent the boundaries of cultivated land. Liddington Castle was one of the favourite haunts of Richard Jefferies, the Victorian naturalist who lived for most of his life in the neighbourhood and wrote extensively about Wiltshire. His friend, the poet Alfred Williams, wrote:

Oft times on Liddington's bare
  peak I love to think and lie,
And muse upon the former day
  and ancient things gone by,
To pace the old castellum walls
  and peer into the past,
To learn the secret of the hills,
  and know myself at last,
To woo Dick Jefferies from his
  dreams on sorrow's pillow
  tossed,
And walk with him upon the ridge,
  and pacify his ghost.

On a concrete plinth on the summit of the hill is a plaque: 'Liddington Hill. The hill beloved of Richard Jefferies and Alfred Williams.' Jefferies' birthplace at Coate on the outskirts of Swindon is now a museum and contains a collection of memorabilia, manuscripts, first editions and letters.

Wanborough, 1¾ miles off the Path, has accommodation.

Foxhill has a public house and a bus service to Swindon and Hungerford.

The Shepherd's Rest, one of the few public houses actually on the line of the Path, is situated at the crossroads at Foxhill. At this point, Ermin Way, the old Roman road from Gloucester to Newbury, crosses the Path.

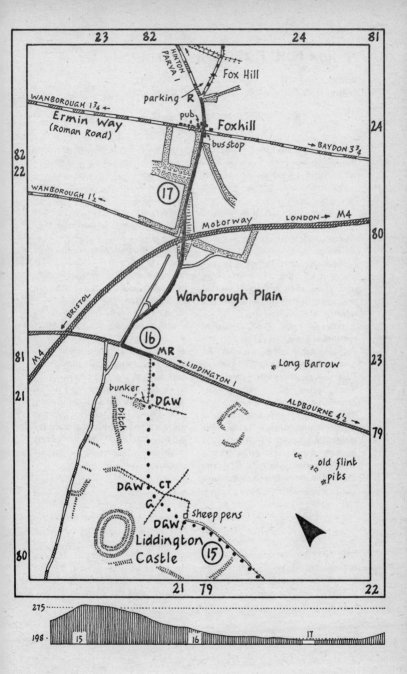

23   82   24   81

HINTON PARVA I

Fox Hill

parking   R

WANBOROUGH 1¾ ←

Ermin Way
(Roman Road)

pub

Foxhill

bus stop   ← BAYDON 3¾

24

82
22

WANBOROUGH 1½ ←

⑰

Motorway   LONDON → M4

80

Wanborough Plain

BRISTOL ←

⑯ MR

M4

← LIDDINGTON I   * Long Barrow

23

81
21

bunker

DAW

Ditch

ALDBOURNE 4½ ←

79

old flint pits

DAW CT

G

□ sheep pens

DAW

Liddington
Castle   ⑮

80

21   79   22

275 ┈┈┈┈┈┈┈┈┈┈┈┈┈┈┈┈┈┈┈┈┈┈┈┈┈┈┈
198 |15| |16| |17|

45

8. Fox Hill, Ridgeway Farm

2 miles
Maps: 1:25000 sheet SU28; 1:50000 sheet 174

Bishopstone, about a mile off the Ridgeway Path, has a post office stores, a public house and accommodation. Early closing day is Saturday.

The parish church of St Mary is mainly Perpendicular in style, although it has an ornate Norman doorway in the chancel and a Norman porch. The local blacksmith made the clock in 1654 and, although it no longer works, the mechanism is still in the tower.

Just off the Path, midway between miles 18 and 19, are some notable strip-lynchets. At one time archaeologists believed that the characteristic platforms were deliberately constructed in pre-Roman times to improve soil drainage and to take advantage of south-facing slopes. It is now generally accepted that the Saxons were responsible for all well-preserved lynchets. It seems likely that only the Saxons had ploughs heavy enough to carve away the hillside and the reason that they did it was not to improve the drainage but was a direct result of the density of settlements and the need to use land as efficiently as possible. Had there been no land hunger, it is unlikely that lynchets would have been constructed. Throughout southern England and especially in Dorset and the North Wessex Downs there are innumerable remains of old field systems, some dating from about 3000 BC, when the first farmers arrived. Many have been destroyed by subsequent ploughing and it takes the eye of an expert to recognize the very faint traces which remain. Aerial photography is the best way of discovering these ancient sites and it is amazing how clearly the remains of old fields will show through modern crops.

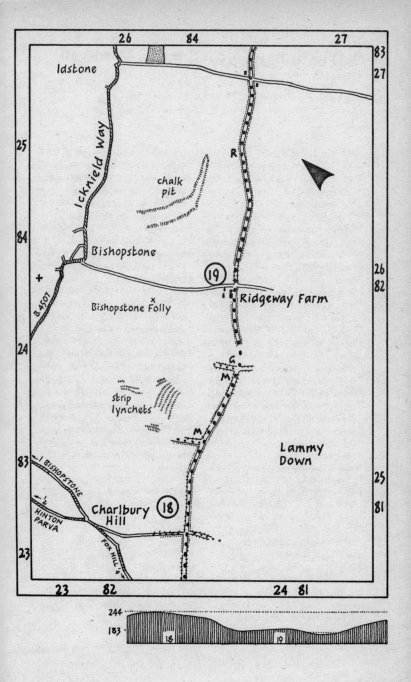

Idstone

Icknield Way

chalk pit

R

Bishopstone

⑲

Bishopstone Folly

Ridgeway Farm

B 4507

+

strip lynchets

G
M

M

Lammy Down

1 BISHOPSTONE

½

HINTON PARVA

Charlbury Hill

⑱

FOX HILL

244

183 ⑱ ⑲

9. B4000, Wayland's Smithy, Hardwell Barn

3 miles
Maps: 1:25000 sheet SU28; 1:50000 sheet 174

Ashbury, ¾ mile off the Path, has a post office store, a public house and accommodation. Early closing is on Wednesday.

It is an attractive chalk-built village which nestles under the Downs. The parish church of St Mary, built of chalk and brownstone, has traces of Norman work but most of the present building dates from the thirteenth century. In the chancel floor are some fourteenth- and fifteenth-century brasses to John de Walden, Thomas de Bushbury and William Skelton. In 1777 the Rev. Thomas Stock founded a Sunday School which was the first to occupy its own separate building. The Manor House, of chalk and stone and dating from the fifteenth century, was probably built by the monks of Glastonbury, who held lands in the area.

Ashdown Park, a National Trust property on the B4000 about 2 miles on the southern side of the Ridgeway Path, was built in about 1660 for the first Earl of Craven. Near-by is Alfred's Castle, a large Iron Age site which was occupied by many different cultures over the years. Alfred the Great is reputed to have used the 'castle' to summon his hosts before the great Battle of Ashdown in 871 which forced the Danes to retreat to Reading.

A gate and a path give access to Wayland's Smithy, a megalithic long barrow in a remarkable state of preservation. It is an enormous tomb dated to about 3000 B C and we must presume that those buried in it had some special regal or sacerdotal importance. The name is derived from the old Saxon legend which declares that Wayland, the Smith of the Gods, would shoe your horse if a penny was left by the barrow. Rudyard Kipling uses the legend in his marvellous story *Puck of Pook's Hill*. It is situated in a stand of trees beside the Ridgeway Path and is 180 ft long and 48 ft wide at the front, tapering to 20 ft wide at the back. It was built in two stages within a short time of each other. Originally a long barrow was constructed to contain 14 skeletons, which were found laid on a platform of sarsen stones and covered by a wooden ridged canopy. Some time later the chambered tomb was constructed from sarsen stones and eight more bodies buried in it. A radio carbon reading suggests a date for the period two-chambered tomb as 2820 B C $\pm$ 130 years. It is probable that the tomb was built by the Windmill Hill people, who also built Avebury, the West Kennett long barrow and Silbury Hill.

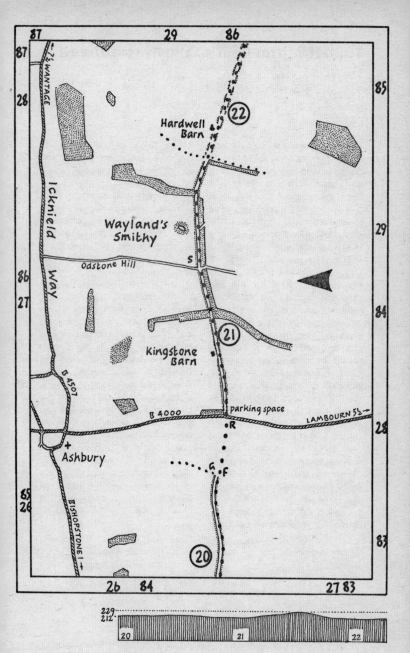

87   29   86

87
28   85

                    Hardwell
                    Barn   22

WANTAGE

Icknield

Wayland's
  Smithy   29
                              S
          Odstone Hill

86
27   84

                        21

        Kingstone
          Barn

B 4507   parking space
              B 4000   LAMBOURN 5½ →
                                    R   28

      Ashbury   G F

85
26   83

BISHOPSTONE 1

                        20

    26   84   27 83

229
212
    20   21   22

10. Uffington Castle, Blowingstone Hill

2½ miles
Maps: 1:25000 sheet SU28/38; 1:50000 sheet 174

Uffington Castle is an Iron Age hill fort consisting of a single rampart with an external ditch and counterscarp bank. It was excavated in the nineteenth century and some post holes were discovered which indicated the existence of a wooden building or shelter within the ramparts.

The near-by White Horse of Uffington cannot be seen from the Ridgeway Path and the best view is obtained from the B4507 road. It is one of the most interesting of all the white horse chalk figures, measuring 365 ft long and 130 ft high. The earliest record of it is in an eleventh-century cartulary of Abingdon Abbey, but it was probably old then. It has been suggested that it may have been constructed to celebrate Alfred's victory over the Danes at the Battle of Ashdown (AD 871), but modern opinion inclines towards the belief that it dates from the Iron Age because of the likeness to horses on coins of the period.

Dragon Hill, a flat-topped hill, to the north, is the reputed site of the slaying of the dragon and the bald patch on the summit is supposed to represent the dragon's blood.

Uffington, 2 miles off the Path, has accommodation.

Kingston Lisle, 1¼ miles off the Path, has a public house and accommodation. The manor belonged to the king, who granted it to Gerard de l'Isle who added his name to it. The parish church of St John the Baptist has a Norman chancel, an early thirteenth-century nave, a Jacobean screen and some traces of wall paintings. It has a most attractive wooden bell turret and spirelet. At the crossroads on the B4507, just outside the village, is a cottage which was once an inn. Under a tree in the garden is a sarsen stone riddled with holes which those who know the secret can blow into, and produce a loud sound. Legend has it that King Alfred summoned his armies to assemble for the Battle of Ashbury by sounding the blowingstone.

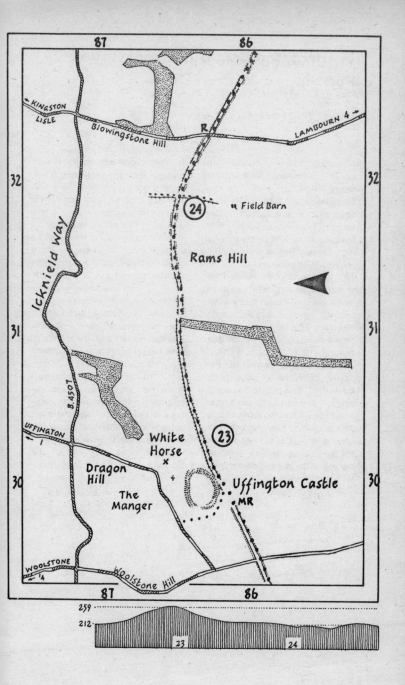

87 86

← KINGSTON
LISLE

Blowingstone Hill R LAMBOURN 4 →

32   32

Icknield Way

(24) « Field Barn

Rams Hill

31   31

B.4507

UFFINGTON
←

(23)

White
Horse
×

Dragon
Hill +

The
Manger • Uffington Castle
    • MR

30   30

WOOLSTONE
←
¼ Woolstone Hill

87 86

259
212

23 24

11. Blowingstone Hill, Devil's Punchbowl, Warren Down

2½ miles
Maps: 1:25000 sheet SU38; 1:50000 sheet 174

Sparsholt, 1¾ miles off the Path, is an attractive village with some half-timbered cottages. The church of Holy Cross has a shingled broach spire, a fourteenth-century chancel constructed from chalk, an interesting Easter Sepulchre, a tomb recess, a sedilia and a piscina. The thirteenth-century wooden screen is a very early example. There are a number of interesting brasses and carved wooden effigies. The near-by red-and-blue-brick Manor House dates from about 1722.

Lambourn, 4 miles off the Path at mile 26, has a grocer's shop, a post office and public houses. As every follower of the turf knows, it is famous for its racing stables. The splendid, springy turf of the downs makes it an ideal centre for the exercising and training of horses. The parish church is a Norman foundation with side chapels added in the fifteenth and sixteenth centuries. In the south transept there is a charming carving of hounds hunting a hare and a bas-relief in alabaster of King Charles I with an angel on each side of him. There are some good brasses dating from the fourteenth century. In the village are some sixteenth-century almshouses built around a court and an ancient cross which stands outside the church. Thomas Hardy used the village as a model for Maryland in his novel *Jude the Obscure*.

In the vicinity of Lambourn there is much evidence of prehistoric activity. To the north are the Seven Barrows (there are actually more than forty!), which date from the Bronze Age, lying in a group in a hollow of the downs.

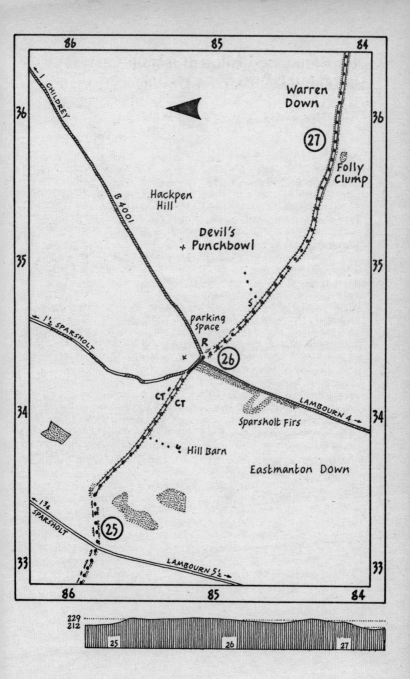

86　　　　　85　　　　　84

36　　　　　　　　　　　　　Warren
↖ CHILDREY　　　　　　　Down

　　　　　　　　　　　　　　　　　27

　　　　　　　　　　　　　　　　　Folly
　　　　　Hackpen　　　　　　　Clump
　　　　　Hill

　　　　　Devil's
　　　　+ Punchbowl

35

B 4001

　　　　　　　parking
　　　　　　　space
↖ 1½ SPARSHOLT　　R
　　　　　　k　　　26

　　　　CT
34　　　　　　CT　　　　　LAMBOURN 4 →

　　　　　　　　　Sparsholt Firs

　　　　　　↙ Hill Barn

　　　　　　　　　Eastmanton Down

↖ 1¾
SPARSHOLT
33　　25

　　　　　　LAMBOURN 5½ →

86　　　　　85　　　　　84

229
212
　　25　　　　　26　　　　　27

53

12. Parsonage Hill, Letcombe Castle, Furzewick Down

$2\frac{1}{2}$ miles
Maps: 1:25000 sheet SU38; 1:50000 sheet 174

Letcombe Bassett ($\frac{3}{4}$ mile off the Path) has accommodation. It gets its name from *Ileda*, a ledge, and *cumb*, a narrow valley. Richard Basset held the manor in 1158 and it remained in the family for several generations. The church of St Michael has been much restored; the chancel is Norman and probably the nave too, but the tower was built in the thirteenth century. Jonathan Swift, a friend of the then vicar, lived in Letcombe Bassett from June to September 1714 before returning to Ireland and wrote *Free Thoughts on the Present State of Affairs* here. It was the model for Cresscombe in Thomas Hardy's *Jude the Obscure*, and Arabella's cottage can still be seen standing isolated among the watercress beds for which the village is famous.

Letcombe Regis ($1\frac{3}{4}$ miles off the Path) has accommodation. It takes its name from the same brook and is distinguished by the addition of 'Regis' to signify that the manor was held by the crown. The church of St Andrew is built on a mound and dates mostly from the thirteenth century, although it possesses a Norman tub font. The village has some attractive thatched cottages one of them bearing the date 1698.

Letcombe Castle (also known as Segsbury Camp) is yet another Iron Age hill fort on the Great Ridgeway. It comprises a single rampart which encloses 26 acres. Around the edge is a deep ditch and, according to an eighteenth-century description, the rampart was faced with sarsen stones. The original entrance was on the eastern side – all other entrances are modern. When excavations took place in 1871 much Iron Age pottery was uncovered together with some pieces of human bones in a cist, flint scrapers and a Saxon shield boss.

The farm opposite Letcombe Castle has a notice stating that water is not available. Before condemning the person responsible for erecting it as unfriendly, walkers should consider that there are very few houses on the line of the Path and that there are thousands of people who walk the route. If only a fraction of that number stopped to ask for water, the life of the farm would be greatly disrupted.

Wantage (3 miles off the route) has a population of 8,500. There are shops, cafés, restaurants, bus services and accommodation. It was the birthplace of King Alfred and is an attractive market town, mainly Georgian in character. The only striking building is the parish church of St Peter and St Paul, which dates mainly from the thirteenth century. The stalls have misericords of various designs, and there are some good brasses.

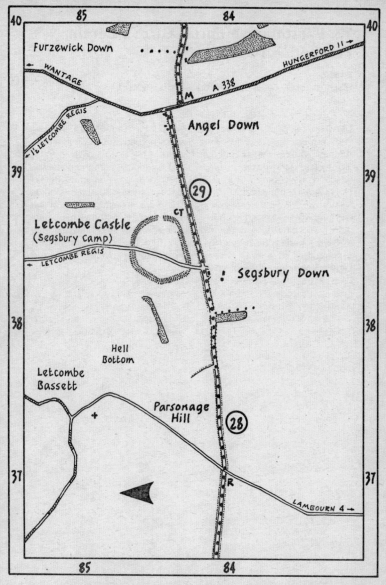

Furzewick Down

WANTAGE

½ LETCOMBE REGIS

A 338

M

Angel Down

HUNGERFORD 11 →

(29)

CT

Letcombe Castle
(Segsbury Camp)

LETCOMBE REGIS

Segsbury Down

Hell
Bottom

Letcombe
Bassett

Parsonage
Hill

(28)

R

LAMBOURN 4 →

229
212

28   29

13. Whitehouse Farm, Grim's Ditch, Wether Down

2 miles
Maps: 1:25000 sheet SU48/58; 1:50000 sheet 174

Between miles 31 and 32 the Path crosses the route of King Alfred's Way. This is another 'unofficial' long-distance path which runs from Portsmouth (King Alfred founded the Royal Navy) via Winchester (his capital) and Wantage (his birthplace), to Oxford (he is reputed to have founded the University). (The guide *King Alfred's Way* by Laurence Main is available from the publisher, the Thornhill Press, 24 Moorend Road, Cheltenham, Glos.)

The imposing monument was erected to commemorate Robert Loyd Lindsay, Baron Wantage VC, KCB, a distinguished soldier who won the Victoria Cross in the Crimean War and who founded the Red Cross Aid Society. He was a great public benefactor.

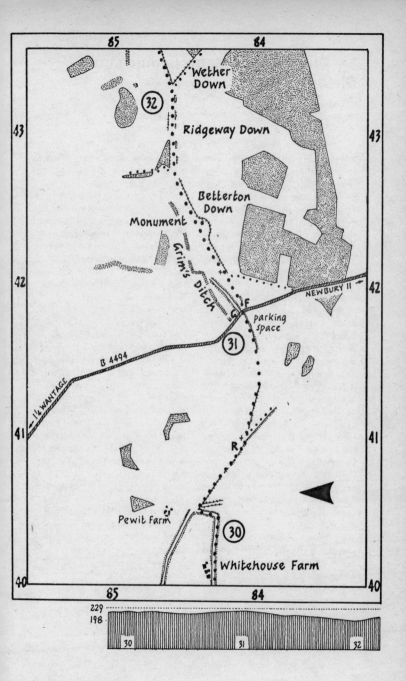

Wether Down

32

Ridgeway Down

Betterton Down

Monument

Grim's Ditch

F

parking space

31

B 4494

NEWBURY 11 →

1¼ WANTAGE

R

Pewit Farm

30

Whitehouse Farm

229
198

30   31   32

14. The Warren, Scutchamer Knob, Sheep Down

2½ miles
Maps: 1:25000 sheet SU48/58; 1:50000 sheet 174

Walkers cannot fail to notice the huge cooling towers of Didcot power station and the brick complex of the Harwell Atomic Energy Research Establishment, both of which can be seen from the curiously named Scutchamer Knob, located in a copse on the southern side of the Path. There is much argument in archaeological circles as to what it is, but in the absence of firm evidence obtained by excavation, modern opinion inclines to the belief that it is an Iron Age barrow which was later used by the Saxons as both a burial mound and as a moot, or meeting place. It has even been suggested that it was the central meeting place of the whole West Saxon kingdom. The name is derived from Cwicchelmshlaew, which means the burial place or law of Cwichelm. We know that Cwichelm was a Saxon king of Wessex, who seems to have spent much of his time fighting, as he is mentioned several times in the *Anglo-Saxon Chronicle*.

A more modern version of Cwichelm's name is to be found in the near-by Cuckhamsley Hill, which is also mentioned in the *Anglo-Saxon Chronicle*. It is described in an event which took place three and a half centuries after the death of Cwichelm when the Saxons were trying desperately to defend Wessex against the marauding Danes:

1006. ... When it drew near to winter the levies (i.e. the Danes) went home, and after Martinmas the host retired to its safe base on the Isle of Wight, procuring everywhere there whatever they had need of. At Christmas they proceeded out through Hampshire into Berkshire to their well-stocked food depot at Reading, and as usual kindled their beacons as they went. They went to Wallingford and burned it to the ground and proceeded along the Berkshire Downs to Cuckhamsley Knob and there awaited the great things that had been threatened, for it had often been said that if ever they got as far as Cuckhamsley Knob, they would never again reach the sea, but they went back by another route. Then [Saxon] levies were mustered there at East Kennett and there they joined battle; but the Danes soon put that force to flight, and bore their plunder to the sea. There the people of Winchester could watch an arrogant and confident host passing their gates on its way to the coast, bringing provisions and treasures from a distance of more than fifty miles inland ...

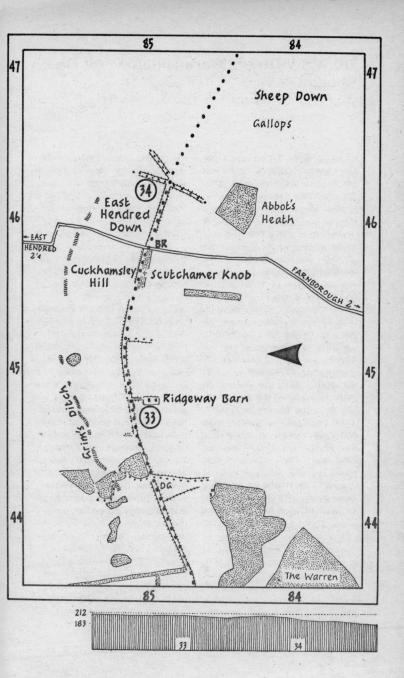

Sheep Down

Gallops

34

East
Hendred
Down

Abbot's
Heath

46

← EAST
HENDRED
2'4

BR

Cuckhamsley
Hill

Scutchamer Knob

FARNBOROUGH 2 →

45

Grim's Ditch

Ridgeway Barn

33

DG

The Warren

212
183

33   34

15. Cow Down, Gore Hill, Several Down

2¼ miles
Maps: 1:25000 sheet SU48/98; 1:50000 sheet 174

Walkers should take great care when crossing the very busy A34, as it is quite wide and traffic travels along it at high speed. The memorial is to 2nd Lieut. Grosvenor, killed accidentally on a training exercise near this spot. Sometimes fresh flowers are placed on this touching, unassuming memorial.

East Ilsley, 2¼ miles off the Path, has a public house and accommodation. It was once the site of an important sheep fair where, during the eighteenth century, as many as 80,000 sheep in a day and 400,000 in a year would be sold. It was held fortnightly from the Wednesday after Easter until the end of the summer. The fair declined in the early years of this century with the development of refrigerated ships and the import of New Zealand lamb. The last was held in 1934.

East Ilsley Hall is an attractive two-storey early Georgian house of red and blue bricks. Stephen Hemsted, who lived there, tried unsuccessfully to interest the women of the village in spinning. He described the village in an amusing piece of doggerel:

Ilsley, remote amid the Berkshire Downs,
Claims these distinctions o'er her sister towns;
For favoured for sheep and wool, tho' not for spinners,
For sportsmen, doctors, publicans and sinners.

The church of All Saints at West Ilsley, 1 mile off the Path, is not particularly interesting and most of it dates from the Victorian era. At one time the village boasted two breweries and the local beer had a very high reputation. Little trace of the industry now remains, although the connection is maintained by the naming of Morland Close after the famous Abingdon brewery.

West Ilsley has a public house and accommodation.

60

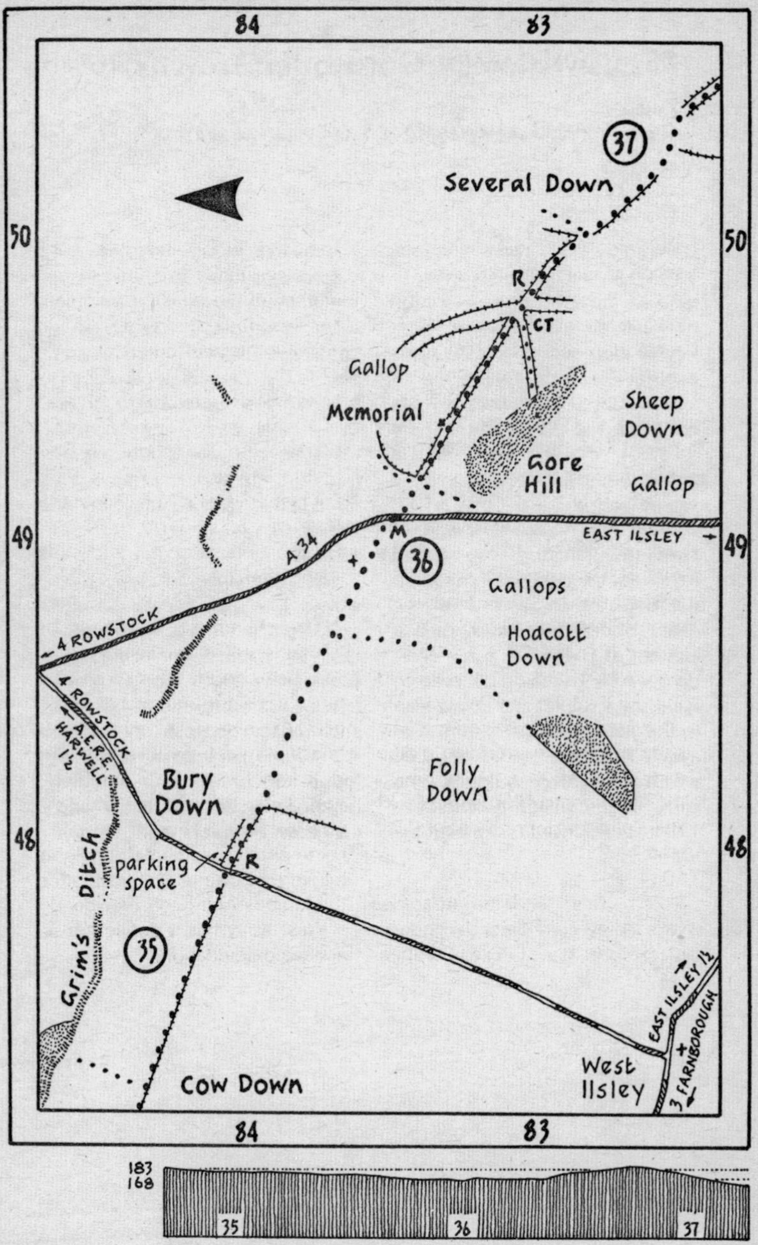

84
83
37
Several Down
50
50
R
CT
Gallop
Memorial
Sheep
Down
Gore
Hill
Gallop
M
EAST ILSLEY
49
49
A 34
36
Gallops
4 ROWSTOCK
Hodcott
Down
4 ROWSTOCK
A.E.R.E.
HARWELL
1½
Folly
Down
Bury
Down
48
48
Ditch
parking
space
R
35
Grim's
EAST ILSLEY 1½
FARNBOROUGH
West
Ilsley
3 FARNBOROUGH
Cow Down
84
83
183
168
35
36
37

16. East Ilsley Down, Roden Downs

$2\frac{1}{2}$ miles
Maps: 1:25000 sheet SU48/58; 1:50000 sheet 174

Compton ($1\frac{1}{2}$ miles off the Path) has accommodation. It is not very attractive and has a large new estate which provides housing for those working at the Agricultural Research Station.

Blewbury, $2\frac{1}{2}$ miles to the north of the Path, has a post office, a grocer's shop and a public house. It is an attractive village and was the home of Sir William Nicholson, R A, and of Kenneth Grahame, who retired here from the post of Secretary to the Bank of England. After the death of his only child, then a student at Oxford, in a rail accident which Grahame believed to have been suicide, he could bear to live here no longer and moved away. Another famous resident was the Rev. Morgan Jones, who came to the village as curate in 1781. He achieved national notoriety as a miser and his death was recorded in the National Register under that heading. He ate and drank very little, unless it was at someone else's expense, and used the stubs of altar candles for lighting. He had a total income of £80 per year, but by careful investment he left an estate of £18,000 and was the model for Blackberry Jones in Charles Dickens's novel *Our Mutual Friend*.

The Ordnance Survey map shows Lowbury Hill as the site of a Roman temple. It is a rectangular banked enclosure approximately 200 ft long and 140 ft wide, dated to about A D 200 and probably occupied until about A D 400. When excavated, it was found to contain two wooden buildings with tiled roofs and may have been a farm.

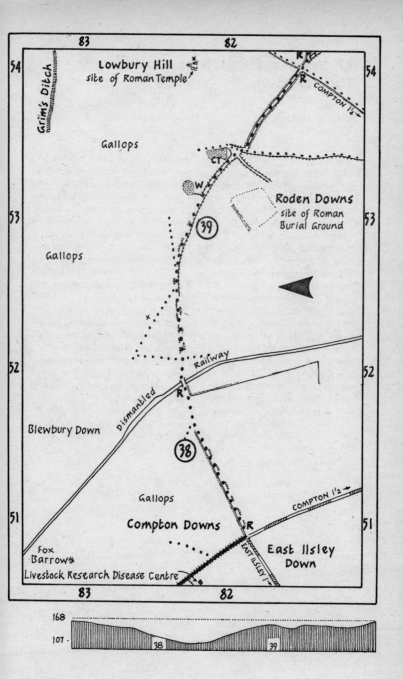

Lowbury Hill
site of Roman Temple

Grim's Ditch

Gallops

CT

W

Roden Downs
site of Roman
Burial Ground

39

Gallops

Gallops

x

Railway

Dismantled

R

Blewbury Down

38

Gallops

Compton Downs

COMPTON 1¼

COMPTON 1½

R

EAST ILSLEY 1⅞

East Ilsley
Down

Fox
Barrow

Livestock Research Disease Centre

168
107

38   39

17. Warren Farm, Streatley Warren, Thurle Down

2 miles
Maps: 1:25000 sheet SU48/58; 1:50000 sheet 174

The Ridgeway now begins the long descent to the Thames. Over the course of many centuries England's most important river has been tamed, the catchment area has been efficiently drained, locks have been built to regulate the flow of water and flooding has been largely eliminated. During the time the Ridgeway was in use as a highway the river was a most formidable barrier. It was much wider than it is now and surrounded by marsh and forest and although there was a ford it must often have been a perilous crossing. It is known that the Romans used the ford between Goring and Streatley (the name Streatley is derived from the Roman *strata*, meaning a

road). In later years there was a ferry and the first bridge was built in 1838. The Thames was for centuries a great highway for shipping and many invaders sailed their boats into the heart of southern England. The only river traffic the modern traveller will see are small pleasure craft.

Aldworth, 1 mile off the Path, once had a yew tree in the churchyard reputed to be 1,000 years old and with a girth of 27 ft. St Mary's has one of the richest collections of fourteenth-century effigies in the whole country, though many of them were mutilated by the Puritans (in this case there is documentary evidence to prove the story).

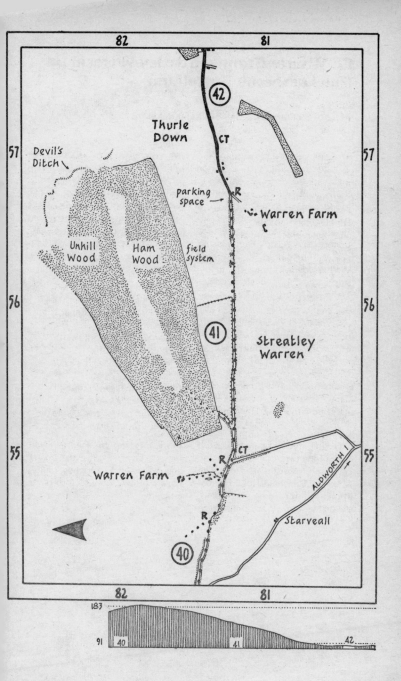

82   81

42

Thurle
Down

CT

57   57

Devil's
Ditch

parking
space   R

Warren Farm

Unhill   Ham
Wood   Wood   field
system

56   56

41   Streatley
Warren

Warren Farm   R   CT

55   55

ALDWORTH 1

R

Starveall

40

82   81

183

91   40   41   42

18. Thurle Grange, Streatley, Goring, The Leatherne Bottell Inn

3 miles
Maps: 1 : 25000 sheets SU48/58 and SU68/78; 1 : 50000
sheets 174 and 175

The twin towns of Goring and Streatley are linked by a bridge and mark the halfway point along the Ridgeway Path. Here will be found shops, accommodation, a bank, post office, buses to Reading and Oxford, and trains to London and Bristol. Early closing day is Thursday in Streatley and Wednesday in Goring. The Riverside Stores is open on Sundays. There is a Youth Hostel in Streatley.

Streatley is an attractive town, largely Georgian in character. There was no bridge linking Streatley with Goring until 1838 and before that date the River Thames was either forded or a ferry operated. In 1674, more than 50 people were drowned when crossing the river from Goring.

Goring has a parish church built in the twelfth century on the site of an Augustinian priory. The Miller of Mansfield Hotel is most attractive. According to legend, the first landlord was a miller from Mansfield named Richard or John Cockell. He built the tavern on land given to him by Henry II or Henry III, who called at the mill while hunting. Unaware of his guest's identity the miller served venison pie poached in Sherwood Forest and asked the king what was in it. According to the ballad:

'Then I think,' quoth our King,
'that it's venison':
'Eche Foole,' quoth Richard, 'full
that you may see;
Never are we without two or
three in the roof
Very well fleshed and excellent
fat;
But I pray thee say nothing
where'er thee go;
We would not for two pence the
King should know.'

In the morning, the king revealed his identity, forgave the miller and, in return for his hospitality, gave him land on which to build a tavern.

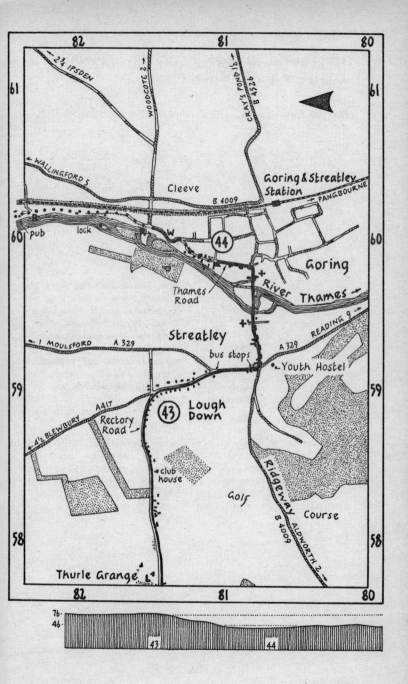

19. Leatherne Bottell Inn, South Stoke, North Stoke

3 miles
Maps: 1:25000 sheet SU68/78; 1:50000 sheets 174 and 178

South Stoke has a public house, a grocer's and bus services to Goring and Wallingford. The shop closes at 12.30 p.m. on Tuesdays. The parish church of St Andrew was constructed in the thirteenth century and enlarged in the following century. There are some wall paintings and some thirteenth-century stained glass. Those with a taste for the by-ways of nonconformity should note the little chapel which they pass on the southern side of the village, originally built in 1820 for the Countess of Huntingdon's Connexion. Selina, Countess of Huntingdon (1707–91), founded the Calvinistic Methodists and was the chief missionary for Methodism among the upper classes. Her belief that, as a peeress, she would appoint to the rank of Chaplain as many Anglican clergy as she wished was disallowed by a consistory court in 1779.

On the Berkshire bank of the Thames can be seen the 400-year-old Beetle and Wedge Hotel. This is the model for the Potwell Inn in H. G. Wells's novel *The History of Mr Polly*, and George Bernard Shaw often stayed here, as he greatly enjoyed rowing. The odd name is derived from the beetle (or hammer) which was used to drive the wedge in the construction of barrels.

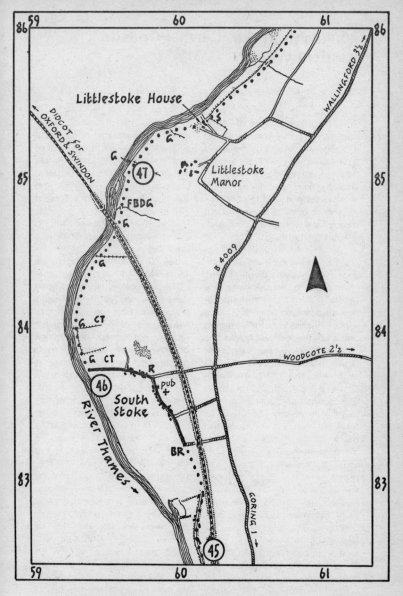

Littlestoke House

DIDCOT for OXFORD & SWINDON

WALLINGFORD 3½

G

47

FBDG

G

Littlestoke Manor

G

G

G

B 4009

G CT

WOODCOTE 2½ →

G CT

R

46

pub

South Stoke

River Thames →

BR

GORING 1

45

4b

45   46   47

20. North Stoke, Carmel College, Icknield Way

3 miles
Maps: 1:25000 sheet SU68/78; 1:50000 sheet 175

From A to B cross from the open field to a small wood by means of a stile. At the end of the wood is another stile and some hen houses. Where the chicken run ends, the path bends slightly right to make for a stile in the church-yard. Walk past the tower and out through the lych gate to the road.

From B to A the route turns up a cul-de-sac leading to the church. Pass through the lych gate and walk through the churchyard round the west side of the tower. Cross the stile in the churchyard wall and pass some hen houses before crossing into a little wood over a stile.

North Stoke has bus services to Goring and Wallingford.

The church of St Mary, North Stoke, dates from the thirteenth and fourteenth centuries. The pulpit is Jacobean. The font dates from the thirteenth century and has a Jacobean cover. Probably the most interesting feature is the series of fourteenth-century wall paintings which depict a doom, the martyrdom of St Thomas a Becket, incidents from the lives of St Catherine of Siena and St Stephen, a passion, and the legend of the living and dead kings. On the south wall of the church is a sundial which has been variously declared by leading experts to be Saxon, Norman and fourteenth-century. The lych gate was donated by Dame Clara Butt, the singer, in memory of her son, who died at Eton College. Dame Clara had a fine voice and was in the habit of singing patriotic songs, her ample figure swathed in the Union Jack, and wearing a helmet and carrying a sceptre to represent Britannia.

From C to D the route through the grounds of Carmel College, a Jewish Public School, is compli-cated. On reaching the grounds by means of a double gate, continue forward along the road past a lake on your right and a telephone box on your left. Where the college drive bears sharply right over some ramps continue forward along the paved bridleway. Just before the paving ends, near a school, turn right over a stile and continue forward, crossing the school drive, to reach the A4074 (cross with care).

From D to C: Cross the A4074 and over the stile 35 yds to the right of the drive leading to Carmel College. Continue for-ward through the wood, crossing a drive which leads to a school, until reaching a stile which gives access to a paved path, turn left and walk to the grounds of Carmel College. Continue for-ward, pass a telephone box on your right and a lake on your left until, at the edge of the grounds, you will see a double gate giving access to a field. Continue for-ward through these gates and head for North Stoke.

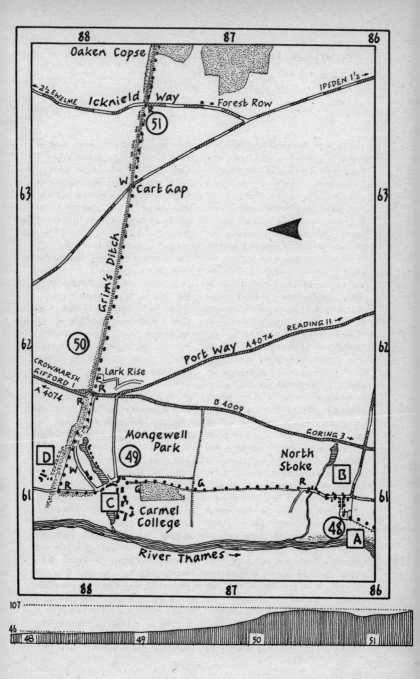

21. Oaken Copse, Nuffield, A423

3 miles
Maps: 1:25000 sheet SU68/78; 1:50000 sheet 175

Along part of Grim's Ditch there are parallel paths, one on the bank and the other in the ditch. The right of way follows the ditch.

Grim's Ditch is one of the many linear earthworks which in some parts of Britain run for miles. Archaeologists are uncertain about their exact purpose, but it seems unlikely that Grim's Ditch was used for defensive purposes, as it runs across flat ground and makes no attempt to take advantage of natural features. A more likely explanation is that it is some kind of boundary. Various suggestions have been put forward, including the possibility that it was part of the enclosure of a large ranch or a territorial boundary. The ranch theory is not attractive because the earthwork does not form an enclosure and some other form of fencing must have existed, to corral the animals. It seems odd that builders should have gone to the immense labour of raising the earthwork when they could much more easily have fenced this part of the enclosure. A territorial boundary seems a much more likely explanation. Perhaps two tribes or kingdoms which had quarrelled for years over grazing rights tired of the fighting, arguments and bloodshed that always surround

such disputes, and decided that the most sensible solution was to mark out a boundary which would be obvious to everyone. Hence a massive earthwork which has lasted well over a thousand years and which makes a splendid vantage point for the modern walker.

Across the golf course (from A to B) the Path is clearly waymarked with white posts. Considerate walkers will avoid treading on the greens and, if a game is in progress, will wait until the golfers have moved away.

The Crown public house a few yards from the Path on the A423 serves delicious snacks.

There is a bus service to Reading and Oxford along the busy A423.

After crossing the A423, westward-travelling walkers should walk up the drive of Fairway Cottage to reach the golf course.

The parish church of Holy Trinity, Nuffield, was built of flint in the thirteenth century and has a Norman font. William Morris, Lord Nuffield, the founder of what is now British Leyland, is buried in a simple grave in the churchyard. Some Christian soul has placed a notice in the churchyard inviting wayfarers to use the water tap in the church wall.

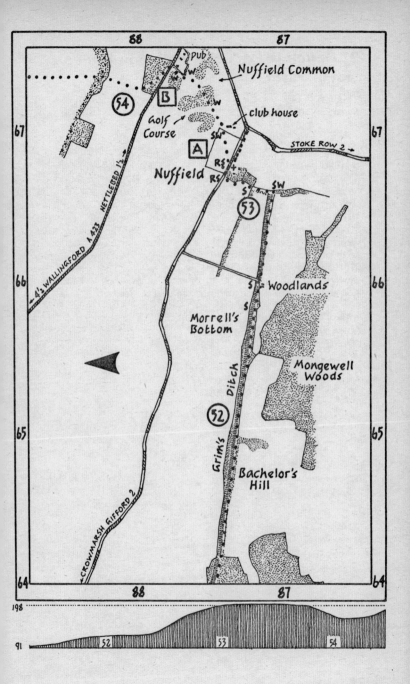

pub
W
Nuffield Common

54

B

Golf
Course

club house

W

SW
STOKE ROW 2 →

A

Nuffield

R⚓

4

R⚓

53

S

SW

S

4½ WALLINGFORD A 423   NETTLEBED 1½

Woodlands

S

Morrell's
Bottom

S

Mongewell
Woods

Ditch

52

Grim's

Bachelor's
Hill

CROWMARSH GIFFORD 2

198

52   53   54

91

22. Ewelme Park, Swyncombe House, North Farm

2½ miles
Maps: 1:25000 sheets SU68/78 and SU69; 1:50000 sheet 175

Ewelme Park, an imposing mansion with beautifully kept grounds, is a replica of the Elizabethan house which stood on this site until it was destroyed by fire in 1913.

Between miles 55 and 56 is a very steep hill which is likely to be muddy and difficult to negotiate after heavy rain. East-bound wayfarers have to turn right along a broad track at the bottom of this hill.

The earthwork midway between miles 56 and 57 is believed to be an ancient boundary.

St Botolph church, Swyncombe, beside the Path, an early Norman church which has neither tower nor steeple, is a very modest building constructed from flint. In the chancel are some fine wall paintings which have been restored, and the rood screen is modern, though medieval in design. The broken thirteenth-century bell is known as the Justice Bell.

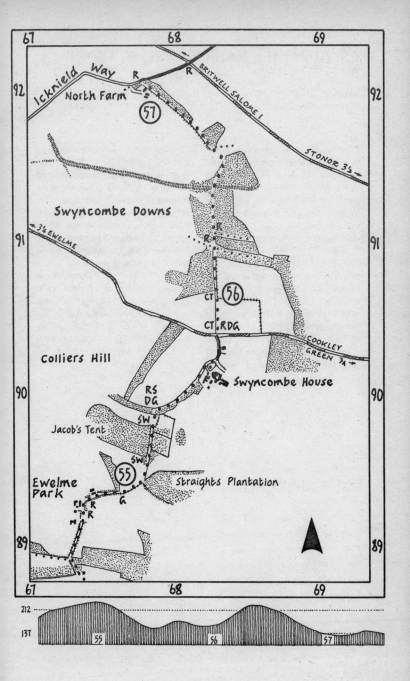

67　　　　　　　68　　　　　　　69

Icknield Way　R　　R　BRITWELL SALOME I
92　　　　　　　　　　　　　　　　　　　　92
North Farm
(57)
　　　　　　　　　　　　　　　　　STONOR 3½ →

Swyncombe Downs

← 3½ EWELME　　　　　　　　R
91　　　　　　　　　　R　　　　　　　91
　　　　　　　　　　　　　　　(56)
　　　　　　　　　CT
　　　　　　　　CT RDG
Colliers Hill　　　　　　　　COOKLEY
　　　　　　　　　　　　　　GREEN ¾ →
　　　　　　　　　RS　　Swyncombe House
90　　　　　　　DG　　　　　　　　90
　　　　　　　SW
Jacob's Tent
　　　　SW
Ewelme　(55)　Straights Plantation
Park
　　　R　G
　　R
89　　　　　　　　　　　　　　　89
67　　　　　　　68　　　　　　　69

212
137　　55　　　56　　　57

75

23. Along the Icknield Way

2½ miles

Maps: 1:25000 sheets SU69 and SU79; 1:50000 sheet 175

Watlington has shops, public houses, a bank, a post office and accommodation. Early closing day is Wednesday. There are bus services to Reading, Oxford, Wallingford and Aylesbury. It is a pleasant market town with a predominantly Georgian air. The parish church of St Leonard was rebuilt in 1877 and only the fifteenth-century tower and a few decorations were retained from the old building. The brick Town Hall was built in 1665 to house the grammar school and market.

The charmingly named Dame Lys Farm, ¼ mile south-west of the B480, is called after Alice of Crowell, who owned the land in 1317.

Between miles 59 and 60 the Path is crossed by the Oxfordshire Way, a 65-mile 'unofficial' long-distance path which runs from Bourton-in-the-Water across Oxfordshire to Henley-on-Thames. This is the brainchild of the Oxfordshire Branch of the Council for the Protection of Rural England, who devised it with the aim of linking the Cotswolds and the Chilterns. (The guidebook *The Oxfordshire Way* by Alison Kemp is available from Sandford Mount, Charlbury, Oxon.)

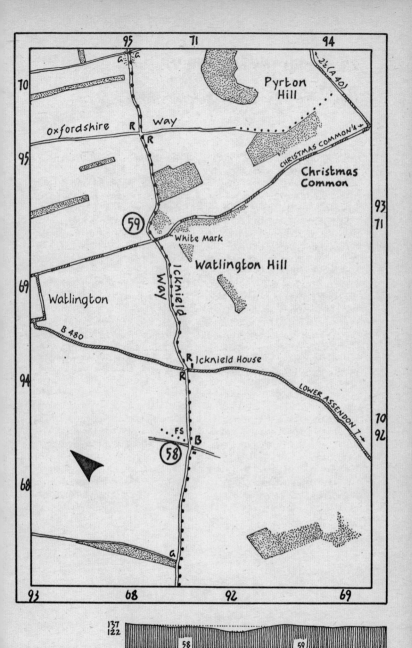

70

95

71

94

G G

Pyrton
Hill

25 (A 40)

Oxfordshire   R   way
              R

CHRISTMAS COMMON 1¼

Christmas
Common

95

93
71

59

White Mark

Watlington Hill

69

Watlington

Icknield   Way

B 480

R Icknield House
R

94

LOWER ASSENDON 7

10
92

FS

B

58

68

G

93

68

92

69

137
122

58   59

77

24. Beechwood, Shirburn Hill, M40, A40

2¼ miles
Maps: 1:25000 sheet SU79; 1:50000 sheet 165

The Path passes underneath the M40 motorway. In the planning stage there was great controversy about this section of the motorway because it was felt that it would ruin the Chiltern escarpment. The planners had their way and, on the whole, it must be admitted that the scars have healed well. Beauty is a subjective matter and many people feel that a railway viaduct often adds to the attraction of the landscape; perhaps one day we shall be able to see that modern motorways do the same.

The Upper Icknield Way is an ancient trackway which probably replaced an earlier route which followed the top of the hills. The Lower Icknield Way, which runs parallel to it, now forms part of the modern road system, and it, too, is very old. Parallel routes so close together strike us as very odd, but it is believed that they may have been used according to the season and weather conditions. After the building of the turnpikes, the Ridgeway and the Icknield Way were used by drovers bringing sheep and cattle from Wales to London.

Shirburn, 1 mile off the Path, has a church dedicated to All Saints and contains some Norman work, although it has been much restored and covered with stucco. The brick castle, which is not open to the public, was built in the late fourteenth century by Worca de Lisle on the site of a moated manor house. It is one of only two castles in Oxfordshire. Although moated, the site does not seem to be very strong and is overlooked by the near-by Shirburn Hill. Thomas Parker, Earl of Macclesfield, bought the estate in 1716 and made extensive alterations to make the castle habitable. It was he who laid out the formal gardens.

On Beacon Hill is a National Nature Reserve designed to protect the typical chalk habitat of the Chilterns.

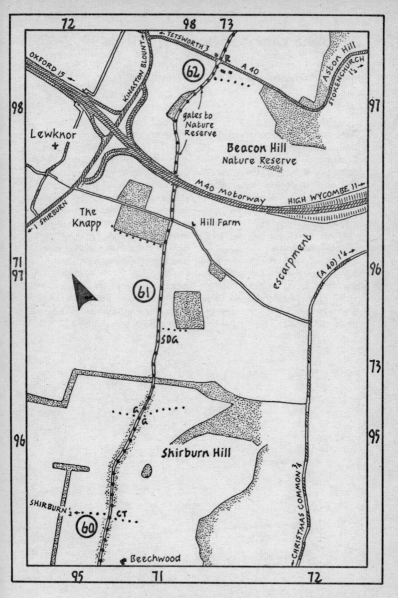

72   98   73

OXFORD 15 ←

← TETSWORTH 3

KINGSTON BLOUNT

62

R   A 40

ASTON Hill

STOKENCHURCH 1½

98

97

Lewknor
+

gates to
Nature
Reserve

Beacon Hill
Nature Reserve

M 40 Motorway

HIGH WYCOMBE 11 →

← 1 SHIRBURN

The
Knapp

◆ Hill Farm

escarpment

(A 40) 1¼

71
97

61

96

SDG

73

95

96

S.
G.

Shirburn Hill

CHRISTMAS COMMON ¾

SHIRBURN ½

CT

60

◆ Beechwood

95   71   72

152

60   61   62

25. A40, Chinnor Chalk Quarries

2½ miles
Maps: 1:25000 sheet SU79; 1:50000 sheet 165

Aston Rowant has accommodation. The parish church of St Peter and St Paul was built by the Normans but has been much restored; there are some good monuments and brasses, including one inscribed in Norman French.

Kingston Blount has a post office stores and a bus service to Watlington and Princes Risborough. Early closing day is Saturday.

Along this stretch of the Path the route runs beside the remains of an old railway which ran from Princes Risborough to Watlington. It was closed to passenger traffic in 1957, although the line is open for freight from Princes Risborough to Chinnor to serve the chalk quarries. The house beside the Path on the road near mile 63 was built for the level-crossing keeper. On Ordnance Survey maps this point is marked as Kingston Crossing.

When the chalk quarries are being excavated, there is a great deal of noise and dust. The chalk is turned into cement for use in the construction industry.

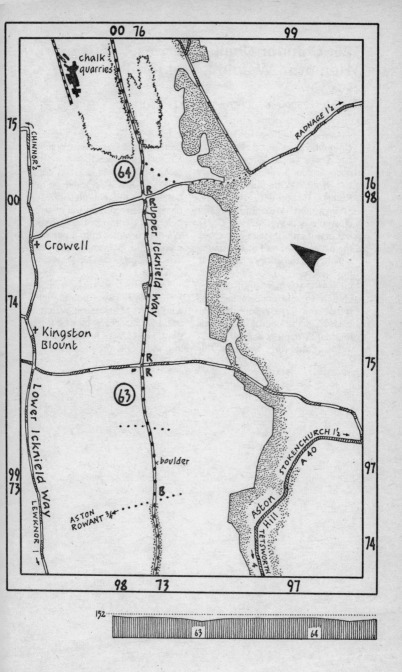

chalk
quarries

CHINNOR 2

RADNAGE 1½ →

64

Crowell

R

Upper Icknield Way

Kingston
Blount

R

R

63

Lower Icknield Way

LEWKNOR 1 →

boulder

B

ASTON
ROWANT ¾ →

STOKENCHURCH 1½ →

A 40

Aston Hill

TETSWORTH 4

00 76   99

75

00

74

99
73

98   73   97

76
98

75

97

74

152

63   64

26. Chinnor Chalk Quarries, Hempton Wainhill, Lodge Hill

3 miles
Maps: 1:25000 sheet SP70; 1:50000 sheet 165

Chinnor, ½ mile off the Path, has shops, a bank, post office, accommodation and bus services to High Wycombe, Oxford, Princes Risborough, Aylesbury, Thame and Watlington. Early closing day is Wednesday. Chinnor is not an attractive town, but the parish church of St Andrew is a gem. It is remarkable because it has escaped restoration and remains a fourteenth-century church entirely uniform in style. It has the largest collection of brasses in the county and some fourteenth-century stained glass.

The Path runs through the garden of Hempton Wainhill House. The notice forbidding the picking of flowers is a sad comment on the way some people behave in the countryside. The name is derived from the near-by hamlet of Henton, or the high ton; Wainhill is either from a personal name, Willa, or from the Old English *wilegn*, meaning willow corner.

East-bound walkers leave the Icknield Way (west-bound walkers join it) at Hempton Wainhill. Within half a mile of this point the Icknield Way is incorporated into the modern road system.

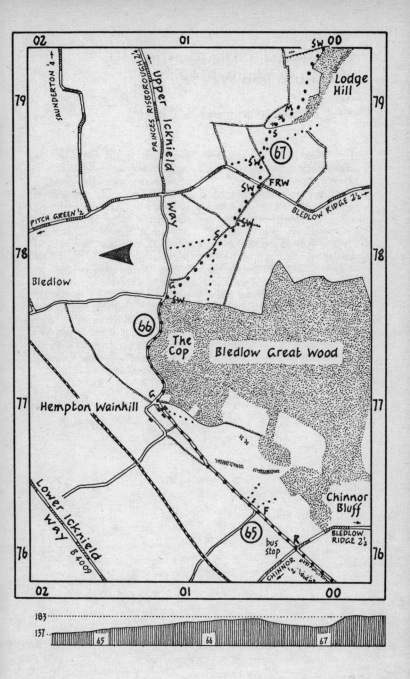

02   01   SW 00

SAUNDERTON '4'

PRINCES RISBOROUGH 2¼

UPPER ICKNIELD

Lodge Hill

79   79

M

S

SW   67

SW   FRW

PITCH GREEN ½

WAY

BLEDLOW RIDGE 2½

SW

S

78   78

Bledlow

S

SW

66

The Cop

Bledlow Great Wood

G

77   77

Hempton Wainhill

Chinnor Bluff

Lower Icknield Way B 4009

F

65   bus stop

R

BLEDLOW RIDGE 2½

CHINNOR AVE ½ 164½

76   76

02   01   00

183 ....

137 ...

65   66   67

27. Lodge Hill, Hemley Hill, Upper Icknield Way

3 miles
Maps: 1:25000 sheet SP80; 1:50000 sheet 165

Great care must be exercised when crossing the railway between miles 68 and 69.

Princes Risborough has shops, banks, a post office, accommodation, a fish and chip shop in Church Street, public houses, trains to High Wycombe, Aylesbury and London and buses to Aylesbury, Bourne End, Longwick, High Wycombe, Thame and Watlington. Early closing day is Wednesday. Princes Risborough is an attractive town with some fine old houses in Church Street. The public library is located in a fifteenth-century yeoman's house which still has some wattle and daub *in situ* although the façade has been rebuilt in brick.

At point A, westward-travelling walkers must resist the natural tendency to walk through the gap in the hedge after crossing the stile. The Path runs past the telegraph pole and through the thicket.

The Upper Icknield Way is joined for a short stretch on either side of mile 70. This is the last that east-bound walkers will see of this ancient route.

West-bound walkers will rejoin the Upper Icknield Way at mile 66 and will then follow it for several miles.

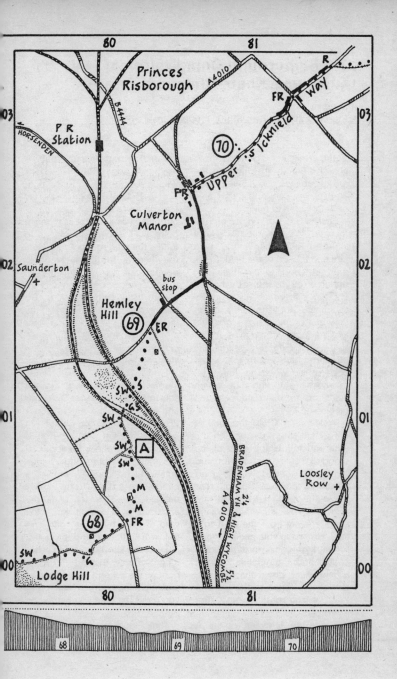

Princes Risborough

HORSENDEN

P R Station

A4010

B4444

R

FR Way

⑦⑩

Upper Icknield

FR

Culverton Manor

Saunderton

bus stop

Hemley Hill

⑥⑨

ER

S

SW

SW

SW

A

SW

M

M

⑥⑧

FR

Loosley Row

BRADENHAM 2¼ & HIGH WYCOMBE 5½

A4010

SW

Lodge Hill

68   69   70

28. Risborough Cop, Whiteleaf Hill, Chequers Knap, Chequers Estate

3 miles
Maps: 1:25000 sheet SP80; 1:50000 sheet 165

Some walkers have experienced difficulty in following the route between the Icknield Way and the car park and picnic area on either side of mile 71:

Eastwards: Turn right off the Icknield Way at the Ridgeway signpost and follow the wire fence to the top of the field. Cross the stile and follow the Path uphill through some bushes to another stile which gives access to a field. Cross the stile and aim diagonally right to make for a stile and signpost which gives access to the road. *Do not cross this stile* but turn sharp left to follow the edge of the wood on your right to another stile and gate which leads on to the road near the picnic site.

Westwards: Cross the road at the picnic site, pass through the gate and follow the edge of the wood to a stile. Continue forward to another stile which gives access to the road. Do not cross on to the road, but instead turn right and walk downhill, moving slightly away from the road to a stile. Cross the stile and continue forward downhill through some bushes and another stile to reach a field. Walk down the field following the fence to the Icknield Way at the bottom, and turn right.

The route between points A and B is complicated. Walkers travelling eastwards should turn left at the road near the pub. A few yards down the road a track will be seen going off to the right near a Ridgeway signpost. This track is not a right of way but is often used as a short cut to reach point B. The correct route is to follow the road for about 200 yds to where a Ridgeway signpost points to a narrow fenced path which emerges on to a field with a well-used path across it. Go through a gap in the hedge on the far side of the field, turn right for a few yards and then left, which will bring you to a stile. Cross the stile and follow the clear path.

From B to A westward-journeying walkers will cross a stile into a sunken lane. Turn right and walk down the lane for about 25 yds and take the overgrown path on the left. At the second stile, continue ahead for about 10 yds, then turn right along a hedge and turn left through a gap in the hedge. Cross the field by a well-defined path to reach a narrow enclosed path which joins the road. Turn left at the road and follow it until reaching the pub.

There is a short cut which is not a right of way. Instead of turning right at the second stile continue straight ahead which will bring you on to the road just below the pub.

The Plough serves delicious snacks and is famous for the variety of cheeses available.

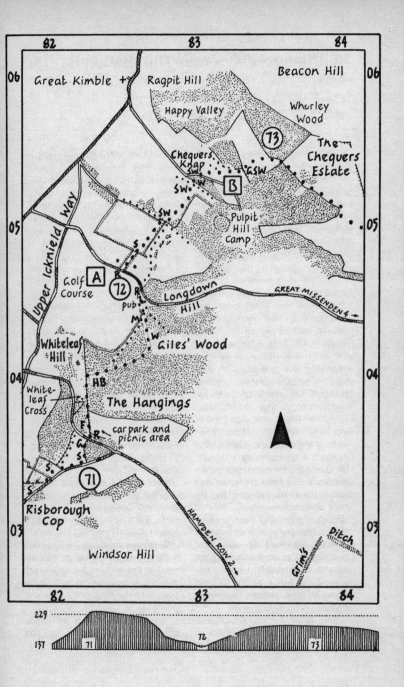

29. Chequers, Coombe Hill, Bacombe Hill

2¼ miles
Maps: 1:25000 sheet SP80; 1:50000 sheet 165

Chequers is the country home of the Prime Minister. Walkers must not be surprised to see the helicopters of visiting statesmen parked in the adjacent fields. When the Prime Minister is in residence, large men in ill-fitting brown suits and wearing boots and bowler hats are to be observed lurking in the woods. The estate is mentioned in the Domesday Book but the present house dates from 1565. Lord Lee of Foreham, the last owner, restored and presented it to the nation in 1922 'as a thank offering for her deliverance in the Great War and as a place of rest and recreation for her Prime Ministers for ever'. Lady Mary Grey, sister of the unfortunate Lady Jane Grey, was imprisoned here in 1565–7 when she incurred the displeasure of Queen Elizabeth I by marrying without first seeking permission from the sovereign. The house is full of art treasures and mementoes, but it is not open to the public.

Walkers travelling east sometimes experience difficulty after crossing the road at mile 74. Continue ahead through the trees along a well-marked path until reaching a broad path which crosses at right-angles. Continue forward, bearing slightly left, climbing up the hill through the trees, and then turn left more sharply to reach the road. This diversion from the original route was sanctioned in 1977 and was waymarked. By peering closely at the trees it may be possible to see some faint evidence of the acorn symbol.

The monument of Coombe Hill, which was erected to commemorate the Boer War, has twice been struck by lightning and severely damaged. Large crowds are likely to be encountered on the top of Coombe Hill on fine summer weekends.

Westward-travelling walkers will find a number of parallel paths when they leave the road in Wendover. They should take the footpath in preference to the bridleway, but if they make a mistake they should not worry, as all paths lead to the top of Coombe Hill.

Daniel Defoe described Wendover as 'a mean, dirty, corporate town' but nowadays it has a handsome Georgian air and is much favoured by commuters. Robert Louis Stevenson stayed at the Red Lion in the High Street and described the pub and the surrounding area in *An Autumn Effect*.

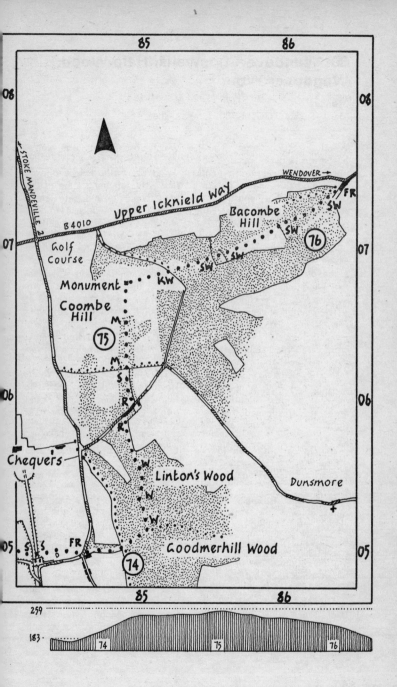

STOKE MANDEVILLE 2

WENDOVER →

Upper Icknield Way

B 4010

Golf Course

Bacombe Hill

FR

SW

SW

SW

SW

(76)

Monument

KW

Coombe Hill

M

(75)

M

S

R

R

Chequers

W

Linton's Wood

W

Dunsmore

W

S S FR

Goodmerhill Wood

(74)

259

183

74   75   76

30. Wendover, Boswells, Hale Wood, Wendover Woods

$3\frac{1}{2}$ miles
Maps: 1:25000 sheet SP80; 1:50000 sheet 165

Wendover (population 3,000), has shops, a bank, a post office, public houses, cafés, restaurants, accommodation, trains to London and Aylesbury and buses to Aylesbury and Halton Camp. Early closing day is Wednesday. The route through Heron Park is complicated and follows the stream. Many walkers prefer to turn right at the roundabout, walk along the A413 and then turn left down the lane leading to the church.

The route between A and B can cause problems. After passing Boswells – a large farm – continue forward along a roughly metalled track. About 75 yds after the rough metalling ends, fork left at Ridgeway Path signpost near an old gatepost. Continue for another 150 yds and then fork right at a waymark and fire beaters.

Lee Gate Youth Hostel (a mile off the Path) can be reached thus:

Eastward-journeying walkers should continue for about $\frac{3}{4}$ mile beyond Boswells to the point where the Path turns sharply left to follow the escarpment. This happens just beyond an old gatepost. Instead of turning left continue forward along a broad forest track with a deciduous wood on the right and conifers on the left. After $\frac{1}{4}$ mile the track forms a T-junction with another track. At this point, turn right and continue forward, ignoring a number of tracks

which cross the path, until reaching a stile on the edge of the wood. Cross the stile and walk down the left-hand edge of the field to a stile and gate which gives access to a track. Turn right along the track for a few yards to reach the road. Turn left and walk along the road for 200 yds to the hostel on the right.

Westward-travelling walkers should turn left about 300 yds beyond the gate near mile 79 at the point where the Path turns sharp right to leave the escarpment and descend into Wendover. The instructions given above now apply.

The route from Lee Gate Youth Hostel to the Ridgeway Path is as follows: On leaving the hostel turn left and walk along the road for 200 yds and turn right up a track by a bridleway sign. After 50 yds turn left and cross a stile beside a gate and follow the right-hand edge of the field to a stile which gives access to a wood. Cross the stile and continue forward for 300 yds, ignoring tracks which cross, until reaching a very broad forest track coming in from the left. Turn left and walk for about $\frac{1}{4}$ mile until the well-used and waymarked Ridgeway Path comes in from the right. Walkers bound for Ivinghoe turn right; those heading for Wendover and Overton Hill continue down the hill.

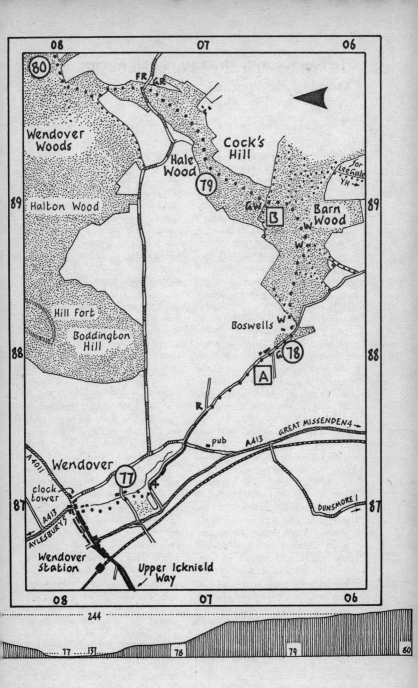

08   07   06

80

FR GR

Wendover Woods

Cock's Hill

Hale Wood

79

89   for Lee hall YH

Halton Wood

G.W.

B

Barn Wood

89

Hill Fort

Boddington Hill

Boswells W.

88   78

A

88

R

pub   A413 GREAT MISSENDEN 4

Wendover

77

A4011

clock tower

87   DUNSMORE 1

87

A413

AYLESBURY 5

Wendover Station

Upper Icknield Way

08   07   06

244

77 131   78   79   80

31. The Crong, Hastoe, Wick Farm

2¾ miles
Maps: 1:25000 sheet SP90; 1:50000 sheet 165

There is a campsite about ¼ mile along the road to Cholesbury at Chivery (*not* Chivery Farm). Walkers travelling east should turn right (those walking westward should turn left) at the road in the bottom right-hand corner of the map near mile 80.

Those walking east must look out for the signposted left-hand turn beyond Wick Farm just before reaching the first houses in Wigginton.

Wick Farm gets its name from William de la Wike, who is mentioned in a Lay Subsidy Roll of 1294 as owning the land.

A section of Grim's Ditch runs parallel to the Path but about ¼ mile to the south. It is as much as 30 ft wide and 10 ft high and is believed to be an Iron Age boundary. Its construction must have imposed considerable strain on the manpower resources of the community who built it.

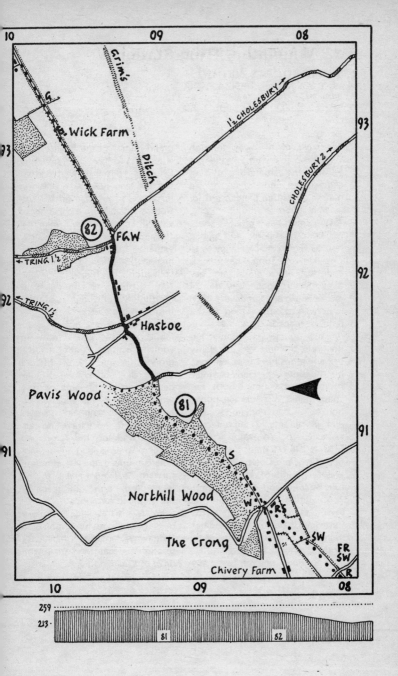

32. Wigginton, Tring Station, Turlhangers Wood

3 miles
Maps: 1:25000 sheet SP91; 1:50000 sheet 165

For most of the way through Wigginton the Path is squeezed between the gardens of a housing estate and a wood which forms a natural adventure playground for small children.

Wigginton has a grocer's shop, a post office stores and public houses. There are bus services to Chesham and Tring. The grocer's and post office stores are, between them, open every day of the week except Sundays.

Between points A and B, the path is fenced; there are some unusual double stiles and a trig point. In the interests of clarity these features have been omitted, but the route is perfectly obvious.

Tring (population 9,500) has shops, banks, a post office, public houses, accommodation, cafés and restaurants. There are bus services to Aylesbury, Little Bushey, Hemel Hempstead, Aldbury, Chesham, Chartridge, Chartwell (via London), Luton, Leighton Buzzard and Halton Camp. Tring station is 2 miles from the town and lies on the route of the Path. It is on the main line and has train services to London, the Midlands, the north and Scotland.

Tring Park, one of the many grand homes of the Rothschilds, is reputed to have been given by Charles II to Nell Gwyn, but what can be seen now is a Victorian mansion. The second Baron Rothschild made a collection of virtually every known mammal (including some species now extinct) and bird and over 2 million butterflies. This amazing collection is housed in the Natural History Museum, just off the High Street, and is open daily throughout the year.

Pendley Manor, in Tring, was rebuilt in 1874 and is now an adult education centre. In the grounds is the site of the old village of Pendley, which was deserted in the fifteenth century when the park was enclosed by Sir Robert Whittingham.

At point C, those travelling east should walk up the farm road leading to Westland Farm and, where it turns to the left, continue forward, walking parallel to the fence on the right, until reaching the gate and turning left.

Westward-travelling walkers must be sure to turn right at a Ridgeway signpost and pass through the gate and on to the drive of Westland Farm.

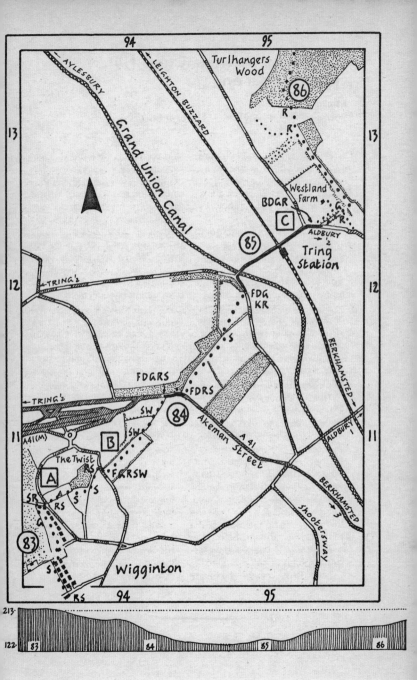

33. Aldbury Nowers, Steps Hill, Ivinghoe Beacon

2¾ miles
Maps: 1:25000 sheet SP92; 1:50000 sheet 165

Eastward-travelling walkers are now on the last lap of their journey. After leaving the wood at Aldbury Nowers, the bare chalk hills of this part of the Chilterns are very reminiscent of the Wiltshire Downs, where the journey began so many miles ago. The only blot on the landscape is the hideous Pitstone cement works.

For those starting their long journey to Overton Hill and Avebury, the Path begins at some pine trees at the road junction and climbs steeply up to the top of Ivinghoe Beacon. Take courage! This is the steepest hill on the whole route.

Ivinghoe has a grocer's shop, a post office store, a public house, a very expensive restaurant, accommodation (including a Youth Hostel and campsite) and buses to Luton and Aylesbury. Early closing day is Wednesday. Ivinghoe has a large and handsome church, dedicated to Saint Mary, which dates from the thirteenth century. On the churchyard wall is a huge firehook which was used for pulling the thatch off burning houses. Next door to the church is the Youth Hostel, a fine eighteenth-century brick building which used to be a brewery, and beyond the Youth Hostel is the old Town Hall, which is probably sixteenth-century although it was rebuilt in 1840. The windmill, dating from 1627, is a post mill and has been so thoroughly restored to working order that occasionally corn is ground in it by volunteers.

On the top of Ivinghoe Beacon is an early Iron Age contour fort.

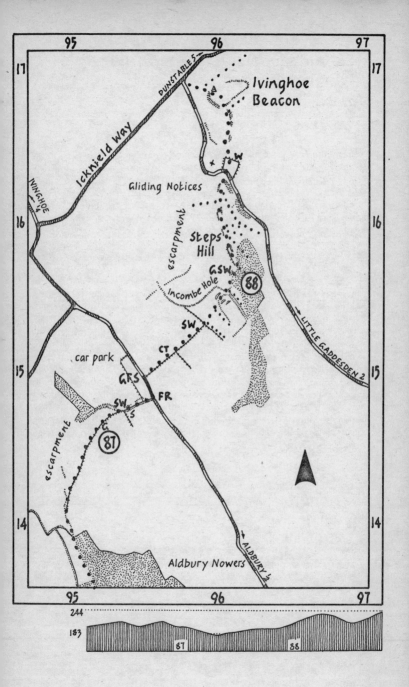

Ivinghoe
Beacon

Icknield Way

IVINGHOE 4

DUNSTABLE 5

Gliding Notices

escarpment

Steps
Hill

GSW

Incombe Hole

88

LITTLE GADDESDEN 2

SW

CT

car park

GFS

SW

FR

S

escarpment

87

Aldbury Nowers

ALDBURY ½

244

183

87

88

Accommodation and Transport

This list of accommodation and transport is arranged in geographical order from west (Overton Hill) to east (Ivinghoe). The nearest mile number on the maps is shown in the entry for ease of reference and to assist in the planning of the walk. Walkers should note that country bus services are subject to change and some services may even be discontinued, and it is advisable to check details with the appropriate bus company:

Chiltern Link (run jointly by Alder Valley and London Country buses): Aylesbury Bus Station, tel. (0296) 84919.

Bristol Omnibus Company: Bus Station, Fleming Way, Swindon, tel. (0793) 22243.

Chiltern Queens: Woodcote, Reading, tel. Checkendon (0491) 354.

London Country Buses: Aylesbury Bus Station, tel. (0296) 84919; Tring Bus Garage, tel. (044 282) 2317.

Oxford–South Midland: Aylesbury Bus Station, tel. (0296) 84919; Gloucester Green Bus Station, Oxford, tel. (0865) 41149.

United Counties: Aylesbury Bus Station, tel. (0296) 84919; Luton Bus Station, tel. (0582) 28899.

Watlington Buses: Brook Street, Watlington, Oxon., tel. (049 161) 2319.

Avebury (2 miles from the start and 1½ miles from mile 2)
Buses: Bristol Omnibus Company service 471 to Swindon and Devizes.

Fyfield (2 miles from the start on the London side of the A4)
Bed and breakfast: Mrs R. McKintosh, Whiteacre, tel. Lockeridge (067 286) 676.

Marlborough (4½ miles from the start on the London side of the A4)
Buses: Bristol Omnibus Company service 470 to Swindon, Ogbourne St George (mile 9) and Savernake Forest.
Bed and breakfast: Mrs M. Mortimer, 23/24 The Parade, tel. (0672) 54410.
Hotels and inns: The Ailesbury Arms, tel. (0672) 53451; The Bear, tel. (0672) 52134; The Castle and Ball, tel. (0672) 52002; The Crown, tel. (0672) 52232; The Green Dragon, tel. (0672) 52366; The Ivy House Hotel, tel (0672) 53188; The Sun Inn, tel. (0672) 52081.

Ogbourne St George (mile 9)
Buses: Bristol Omnibus Company service 470 to Swindon, Marlborough and Savernake Forest.
Bed and breakfast: The Post Office, tel. (067 284) 201.

Aldbourne (4 miles off the Path at mile 13)
Bed and breakfast: The Crown, tel. Marlborough (0672) 40214.

Liddington (1 mile off the Path at mile 16)
Bed and breakfast: The Bell Inn, tel. Wanborough (079 379) 314.

Chiseldon (2 miles off the Path at mile 16)
Bed and breakfast: Mrs D. Cornfield, 5 High Street, tel. Swindon (0793) 740413.

Wanborough ($1\frac{3}{4}$ miles off the Path at mile 17)
Bed and breakfast: The Brewer's Arms, tel. (079 379) 793338.

Foxhill (mile 17)
Buses: Bristol Omnibus Company service 469 to Swindon and Hungerford (no Sunday service).

Ashbury ($\frac{3}{4}$ mile off the Path at mile 21)
Bed and breakfast: The Rose and Crown, tel. (079 371) 222.

Uffington (2 miles off the Path at mile 23)
Buses: Oxford–South Midland service 362 to Kingston Lisle, Letcombe Bassett and Wantage (no Sunday service).
Bed and breakfast: Mrs P. Liddiard, Church Farm, Baulking, tel. (036 782) 305.

Kingston Lisle ($1\frac{1}{4}$ miles off the Path at mile 24)
Buses: Oxford–South Midland service 362 to Uffington (mile 23), Letcombe Bassett (mile 28) and Wantage (no Sunday service).
Bed and Breakfast: The Plough Inn, tel. Uffington (036 782) 288.

Letcombe Bassett ($\frac{3}{4}$ mile off the Path at mile 28)
Buses: Oxford–South Midland service 362 to Uffington (mile 23), Kingston Lisle (mile 24) and Wantage (no Sunday service).
Bed and breakfast: Mrs Leggett, Arabella's Cottage, tel. Wantage (023 57) 4782; The Post Office, tel. Wantage (023 57) 2158.

Letcombe Regis ($1\frac{3}{4}$ miles off the Path at mile 29)
Bed and breakfast: Mrs S. Reade, The Old House, tel. Wantage (023 57) 4437.

Wantage (3 miles off the Path at mile 29 and $2\frac{3}{4}$ miles at mile 31)
Buses: Oxford–South Midland service 362 to Letcombe Bassett (miles 28), Kingston Lisle (mile 24) and Uffington (mile 23). No Sunday service.
Bed and breakfast: The Royal Oak Inn, Newbury Street, tel. (023 57) 3129.

West Ilsley (1 mile off the Path at mile 35)
Bed and breakfast: The Harrow, tel. East Ilsley (063 528) 260.

East Ilsley ($2\frac{1}{4}$ miles off the Path at mile 36)
Hotel: The Swan, tel. (063 528) 238.

Chilton (2 miles off the Path at mile 36)
Hotel: Horse and Jockey Hotel, tel. Abingdon (0235) 834376.

Compton (1½ miles off the Path at mile 38)
Bed and breakfast: Mrs M. Jarrett, the Forge House, tel. (063 522) 387.
Hotel: The Swan Hotel, tel. (063 522) 269.
Streatley (mile 43)
Buses: Oxford–South Midland service 5 to Reading and Oxford.
Bed and breakfast: Mrs P. J. Webber, Bennett's Wood Farm,
Southridge, tel. Goring (0491) 872377; Coombe House, tel. Goring
(0491) 872174.
Hotel: The Swan, tel. Goring (0491) 873747.
Youth Hostel: Hill House.
Goring-on-Thames (mile 44)
Buses: Chiltern Queens to South Stoke (mile 46), North Stoke (mile
48) and Wallingford (no Sunday service).
Trains: to London (Paddington) and Bristol, tel. (0491) 872822.
Bed and breakfast: Mrs H. Hudson, 18 Lockstile Way, tel. (0491)
873872; Leyland Guest House, 3 Wallingford Road, tel. (0491)
872119.
Hotels: The Grange, Manor Road, tel. (0491) 872853; The John
Barleycorn, Manor Road, tel. (0491) 872509; The Miller of
Mansfield, High Street, tel. (0491) 872829; The Sloane Hotel, tel.
(0491) 872668.
South Stoke (mile 46)
Buses: Chiltern Queens service to Goring (mile 44), North Stoke
(mile 48) and Wallingford (no Sunday service).
North Stoke (mile 48)
Buses: Chiltern Queens service to Goring (mile 44), South Stoke
(mile 46) and Wallingford (no Sunday service).
Wallingford (1 mile off the Path at mile 49)
Buses: Chiltern Queens service to North Stoke (mile 48), South
Stoke (mile 46) and Goring (mile 44); Oxford–South Midland
service 5 to Streatley (mile 43), Oxford and Reading.
Hotel: The George, tel. (0491) 36665.
Campsites: There are two campsites near the river.
Nuffield (mile 53)
Buses: Oxford–South Midland service 390 to London and Oxford.
Watlington (¾ mile off the Path at mile 58)
Buses: Oxford–South Midland service 201/2 to Oxford; Watlington
Buses to Nettlebed and Reading.
Bed and breakfast: Mrs M. Roberts, The Cross, High Street, tel. (049
161) 2218; The Well House Restaurant, High Street, tel. (049 161)
2025.
Aston Rowant (¾ mile off the Path at mile 63)
Buses: Oxford–South Midland service 290/790 to Oxford, High
Wycombe and London.
Bed and breakfast: Beacon Cottage Country Guest House, Aston
Hill, tel. Kingston Blount (0844) 51219.
Hotel: The Lambert Arms Hotel, tel. Kingston Blount (0844) 51496.

Kingston Blount ($\frac{1}{2}$ mile off the Path at mile 63)
  Buses: Chiltern Link service 331 to High Wycombe, Chinnor (mile 65) and Thame.
Chinnor ($\frac{1}{2}$ mile off the Path at mile 65)
  Buses: Chiltern Link service 331/2 to High Wycombe, Kingston Blount (mile 63) and Thame; Oxford–South Midland service 232 to Oxford, High Wycombe and Thame.
  Bed and breakfast: The Black Boy, tel. Kingston Blount (0844) 51455.
Princes Risborough ($\frac{1}{2}$ mile off the Path at mile 70)
  Buses: Chiltern Link service 321 to Bradenham (Youth Hostel) and High Wycombe; service 323/4 to High Wycombe, Bradenham (Youth Hostel) and Aylesbury.
  Trains: to London (Marylebone), High Wycombe and Aylesbury, tel. (0844 4) 4467.
  Bed and breakfast: The Black Prince, Wycombe Road, tel. (0844 4) 5569; The George and Dragon, High Street, tel. (0844 4) 3087.
  Youth Hostel: at Bradenham 4 miles along the A4010 (good bus service).
Wendover (mile 77)
  Buses: United Counties service 565/6 to Aylesbury and Halton Camp.
  Trains: to London (Marylebone) and Aylesbury, tel. Aylesbury (0296) 623112.
  Bed and breakfast: Mrs Y. MacDonald, 46 Lionel Avenue, tel. Aylesbury (0296) 623426.
  Hotels: The Red Lion, High Street, tel. Aylesbury (0296) 622266; The Shoulder of Mutton, Pound Street, tel. Aylesbury (0296) 623223; The Vine Tree House Hotel, tel. Aylesbury (0296) 622797.
Lee Gate (1 mile off the Path at mile 78)
  Youth Hostel: Swan Bottom Road.
Wigginton (mile 82)
  Buses: London Country Buses service 394 to Tring (mile 84), Chartridge and Chesham (no Sunday service).
Tring (1 mile off the Path at mile 84)
  Buses: London Country Buses service 304 to Aylesbury and Little Bushey (no Sunday service); service 312 to Hemel Hempstead; service 387 to Tring Station (mile 85) and Aldbury (1$\frac{1}{2}$ miles off the Path at mile 87) (no Sunday service); service 394 to Wigginton (mile 83), Chartridge and Chesham (no Sunday service); London Transport Green Line service 706 to London and Aylesbury; United Counties service 61 to Aylesbury, Ivinghoe (mile 88); service 560/1 to Aylesbury (no Sunday service).
  Trains: to London (Euston) and the Midlands, tel. (044 282) 2128.
  Hotels: The Rose and Crown, High Street, tel. (044 282) 4071; The Royal Hotel, Station Road, tel. (044 282) 2169.

Ivinghoe (1¼ miles off the Path at mile 88)
Buses: United Counties service 61 to Luton and Aylesbury; service
560/1 to Aylesbury (no Sunday service).
Campsite: The Silver Birch Café, Pitstone, tel. Aylesbury (0296)
668348.
Youth Hostel: The Old Brewery House.

Index of Place Names

Index

More About Penguins
and Pelicans

Published in Penguin Handbooks

The Walker's Handbook

Second Enlarged Edition

H. D. Westacott

Maps, Tents, Clothes, Rights of Way, National Parks, The Law, Hostels, Farmers, Gamekeepers, Shoes, Boots, Safety and First Aid – all you need to know to walk safely and happily, whether you take the low road or the high road. This new and enlarged edition also includes extra chapters on challenge walks and walking abroad.

The Complete Book of Running

James E. Fixx

'This book is a boon and a blessing to the multitudes who jog and run throughout the world' – Michael Parkinson.

As the title says, this is The Complete Book of Running, the best book yet written on running for those who run, would like to run, have ever run or are just curious about running.

Fixx explains why runners feel better, live longer, enjoy a more vigorous life, sleep better and smoke and drink less than their sedentary friends. This is the complete book, and so is of use to the beginner and the experienced runner alike. Anecdotal and filled with information, the book contains advice for runners of all ages, men, women and children. Here is the guide to all running, from first steps to total fitness.

Everest

Walt Unsworth

Here Walt Unsworth relates the climbing history of Everest in a new and revealing way. The truth is told about many of the world's mountaineering heroes – about the bumbling, incompetence and rages as well as the courage, endurance and skill commonly thought to characterize the climbing breed. Looking critically (and often wittily) at the people who have tried, failed and succeeded in getting to the top, at their adventures and at the public's response, the author not only reduces the heroes to human dimensions, but makes their achievements both more credible and, above all, even more impressive than before.

Nanga Parbat Pilgrimage

Hermann Buhl

Hermann Buhl was one of the greatest and toughest solo climbers of all time.

Driven on by his enormous determination, he attempted and achieved climbs of such notorious difficulty that he became a legend. The greatest of these was the conquering of Nanga Parbat – an impressive 27,000 feet of sheer rock and ice with a disastrous history of fatalities – when Hermann Buhl ascended the final 3,000 feet on his own and spent the night wedged into a rock crack.

This is his autobiography, which has been out of print for many years. It tells of his life up to and including that famous climb, and brings the flavour of the man and his chosen life, as well as the feel of the mountainside, excitingly to life.